TRUMP CORRECTED

A COUNTER-QUOTATION BOOK

EDITED BY BILL ADLER JR.

Published by Claren Books, www.clarenbooks.com

ISBN: 978-1-945259-10-4

Dedicated to The Resistance and all who support the rule of law, equality, and honesty.

A big thing we have with China was, if they could help us with North Korea, that would be great. They have pressures that are tough pressures, and I understand. And you know, don't forget, China, over the many years, has been at war with Korea—you know, wars with Korea. It's not like, oh, gee, you just do whatever we say. They've had numerous wars with Korea.

—Donald Trump aboard Air Force One, July 12, 2017

War is what happens when language fails.

—Margaret Atwood

They didn't put themselves down as neo-Nazis. And you had some very bad people in that group. But you also had people that were very fine people on both sides.

Remarks about the white supremacist and neo-Nazi march in Charlottesville, Virginia in which one person was killed and nineteen injured, August 16, 2017

"Are you a communist?"
"No I am an anti-fascist"
"For a long time?"
"Since I have understood fascism."

—Ernest Hemingway, *For Whom the Bell Tolls*

The FAKE NEWS media (failing @nytimes, @NBCNews, @ABC, @CBS, @CNN) is not my enemy, it is the enemy of the American People!"

Tweet, February 17, 2017

> The Founding Fathers gave the free press the protection it must have to bare the secrets of government and inform the people.
>
> Supreme Court Justice Hugo Black

Table of Contents

Introduction

Donald Trump, the 45th President of the United States, thinks he is the first and last word on any subject. Donald Trump believes wisdom courses through his veins, and he's the smartest person in the room.

And yet, he's not.

Trump Corrected is a collection of quotations by Donald J. Trump paired with quotations from people who are smarter and wiser than Trump—admittedly not a difficult bar.

Imagine if John F. Kennedy, Martin Luther King, Jr., or Albert Einstein could have corrected Donald Trump's weird, mental concoctions. In *Trump Corrected: A Counter-Quotation Book*, that's exactly what they do. Trump's words are paired with thoughts from presidents, scientists, writers, artists, musicians, businesspeople, philosophers, actors, and others for whom coherence and rationality are important. Great thinkers have a great deal to say about Mr. Trump.

When the Republican-controlled Senate failed to pass a healthcare bill for the second time, Trump said, "I am not going to own it." By contrast, President Harry S. Truman, famous for accepting responsibility, had a sign on his desk that read, "The buck stops here." When Albert Einstein said, "The difference between stupidity and genius is that genius has its limits," he could very well have been talking about Donald Trump's May 2013 tweet, "Sorry losers and haters, but my I.Q. is one of the highest—and you all know it! Please don't feel so stupid or insecure, it's not your fault."

Stephen King wrote, "The trust of the innocent is the liar's most useful tool" in his book *Needful Things*, but he may have been foretelling the rise of Donald Trump who once claimed, "In addition to winning the Electoral College in a landslide, I won the popular vote if you deduct the millions of people who voted illegally."

The ignorance, bigotry, sexism, callousness, pure meanness, idiocy, and kerosene-laden danger of Trump's words becomes especially clear when placed next to words of somebody thoughtful, intelligent, and sensible.

In selecting the counter-quotations for *Trump Corrected*, I looked for positive, enlightening, and enriching words, rather than quotations that merely insulted or contradicted Trump. (That would have been too easy.) My mantra for compiling this book was Michelle Obama's guidance: "When they go low, we go high."

It was often difficult to choose in which chapter to put a particular quotation. Take Trump's utterance on global warming made during a campaign rally: "Obama's talking about all of this with the global warming and . . . a lot of it's a hoax. It's a hoax. I mean, it's a money-making industry, okay? It's a hoax, a lot of it." Should that go in the science chapter? The campaign chapter? Or the chapter on words and language because this sentence reads like it's made up of English language words that don't get along with each other.

Editing *Trump Corrected* required that I read a lot of Donald Trump's speeches, tweets, books and interviews, an experience that caused me to decorate my desk with a bottle of Tums. He's said and written a lot, little of which summoned warm and fuzzy feelings. (But unlike many other presidents and world leaders who write their own speeches, books, and opinion pieces, Trump has written almost nothing longer than 140 characters by himself.) If you were to ask me which is the worst of all Trump's utterances and tweets, I'd skip right to this from a 1990 Playboy Magazine interview:

> *When the students poured into Tiananmen Square, the Chinese government almost blew it. Then they were vicious, they were horrible, but they put it down with strength. That shows you the power of strength. Our country is right now perceived as weak, . . . as being spit on by the rest of the world.*

Out of the mouth of the future President of the United States comes a chilling admiration for brutal government repression. Although Trump said this in 1990, his authoritarian views have remained steadfast.

Trump refused to explicitly condemn white supremacist violence after Heather Hyer was killed by white supremacists in Charlottesville, Virginia in August 2017. Instead, he said, "We condemn in the strongest possible terms this egregious display of hatred, bigotry and violence on many sides—on many sides. It's been going on for a long time in our country. Not Donald Trump, not Barack Obama. It's been going on for a long, long time. It has no place in America." *On many sides.* Trump repeated that phrase, as if that repetition made it true.

Trump acts as if he wishes he were king. He's shown disdain for the rule of law and has boldly equated patriotism with loyalty, as in this July 23, 2017 tweet: "It's very sad that Republicans, even some that were carried over the line on my back, do very little to protect their President."

Writers and politicians share something in common. We're both storytellers. Let me tell you a short story to give some insight into how Trump terrifies us, and how, no matter what, Trump is not the end of the world.

When I was 10 years old, I went to summer camp in Maine. Pine-scented forests, lake swimming, campfires, and chipmunks scurrying all over made camp a wondrous place for a New York City kid who lived most of the year surrounded by concrete and car horns.

The problem was nighttime. I knew there were foxes, moose, bears, and other animals in the woods, and I was okay with that. What scared me were all the creatures that I didn't know about, especially the ones that came out at night—the monsters that lived in the deep woods, the ancient things that enjoyed hearing children scream and chewing on their bones.

My plan every night was to be the first kid asleep, and definitely never the last. I didn't want to be the only person awake, the only one aware and listening for the demons and ghosts that were creeping closer to my cabin. I didn't want to be the only kid who felt the cold breath of death in the last moment of life. The monsters would first want to kill whoever was awake because the monsters enjoy tormenting as much as they enjoy consuming human flesh.

Tree branches scratching against my camp cabin's roof were the anti-sleep. Stormy nights with bellowing thunder that masked the monster's approaching footsteps were even worse.

My plan rarely succeeded, and most nights I was scared and all alone.

Fast forward to perilous 2017. I dread the damage that Donald Trump will do to the environment, civil rights, women's rights, the economy, and the American ideals of equality and liberty. When I think about how Trump, with his pin-sized experience and wisdom, might handle a crisis of war and peace, I want to hide on another planet.

But what holds me together, what keeps me from canceling my newspaper subscription, turning off the Internet, and staying under the bedcovers all day, is that my fear is shared by billions of people. The majority of voting Americans voted against Trump. It's fair to say that the majority of the planet doesn't like him and would give him a vote of no confidence. According to a June 27, 2017 survey, only 22 percent of the global population believes that Trump will do the right thing when it comes to international affairs. I'm not awake all by myself at night, alone, surrounded by the haunted forest.

I'm going to exercise my author's prerogative and create a new aphorism inspired by Donald Trump: "Those who do not learn history are doomed to destroy it."

The Press

I made the chapter about Trump's utterances about the press the book's first chapter because a free press is vital to democracy and because Trump spends so much time trying to discredit and destroy newspapers, television news, and individual reporters. He speciously calls every publication that dares to question him "fake news" and has called for changes to libel laws to make it easier to sue newspapers.

Vice News exposed that twice a day Trump's staff delivers a folder of good, positive, slap-you-on-the-back news. Trump gets anxious and angry with real news, so his staff brings him, according to a staffer, "screenshots of positive cable news chyrons . . . admiring tweets, transcripts of fawning TV interviews, praise-filled news stories, and sometimes just pictures of Trump on TV looking powerful."

All presidents have a love-hate relationship with the press. All presidents, except for Trump, know that the press—newspapers in previous centuries, television and Internet media now—are as important to democracy as the three pillars of government: the President, Congress, and the courts. John F. Kennedy's words about the media summarize how America's presidents should, and mostly have, regarded the press: "I think it is invaluable. It is never pleasant to be reading things frequently that are not agreeable news, but I would say it is an invaluable arm of the presidency as a check really on what is going on in administration. . . . Even though we never like it, and even though we wish they didn't write it, and even though we disapprove, there isn't any doubt that we could not do the job at all in a free society without a very, very active press."

No president has condemned and demonized the media and the truth itself like Trump does. It's almost as if President Trump wants to take a pair of scissors to the First Amendment. At a press conference on August 16, 2017, Trump directly called a reporter "fake news" as if that were the reporter's name.

Trump certainly disagrees with Theodore Roosevelt, who said, "To announce that there must be no criticism of the president, or that we are to stand by the president, right or wrong, is not only unpatriotic and servile, but is morally treasonable to the American public." Trump's February 17, 2017 tweet is as chilling as it is anti-democratic:

> *"The FAKE NEWS media (failing @nytimes, @NBCNews, @ABC, @CBS, @CNN) is not my enemy, it is the enemy of the American People!"*

When Trump declares the press the enemy, he goes to war with what makes America a great democracy.

The FAKE NEWS media (failing @nytimes, @NBCNews, @ABC, @CBS, @CNN) is not my enemy, it is the enemy of the American People!"

Tweet, February 17, 2017

> The Founding Fathers gave the free press the protection it must have to bare the secrets of government and inform the people.
>
> Supreme Court Justice Hugo Black

Fake News CNN is looking at big management changes now that they got caught falsely pushing their phony Russian stories. Ratings way down!

Tweet, June 27, 2017. Trump commandeered the meaning of "fake news" to make the expression his principle propaganda weapon. Fake news is a story deliberately manufactured for financial gain to draw readers in for advertising click revenue, or as a purposeful effort to deceive.

> When the public's right to know is threatened, and when the rights of free speech and free press are at risk, all of the other liberties we hold dear are endangered.
>
> Senator Christopher Dodd

The #AmazonWashingtonPost, sometimes referred to as the guardian of Amazon not paying internet taxes (which they should) is FAKE NEWS!

Tweet, June 28, 2017. Amazon pays taxes—and there's no such thing as an "internet tax."

> Were it left to me to decide whether we should have a government without newspapers, or newspapers without a government, I should not hesitate a moment to prefer the latter. But I should mean that every man should receive those papers and be capable of reading them.
>
> Thomas Jefferson

The FAKE MEDIA is trying to silence us—but we will not let them.

Tweet, July 2, 2017

> War is peace. Freedom is slavery. Ignorance is strength.
>
> George Orwell

We are believers, giving citizens of our country to hear directly from the elected leaders and from us to hear directly from there.

Speaking about social media with Indian Prime Minister Modi, June 26, 2017 in Washington, DC. Trump's message is often muddled by fuzzy thinking and even more unsound language.

> Caesar is not above the grammarians.
>
> Tiberius, Roman Emperor (42 BCE to AD 37)

The media can attack me, but where I draw the line is when they attack you, the decency of our supporters. You are honest, hard-working, tax-paying—and you're over-taxed, but we're going to get your taxes down—Americans. It's time to expose the crooked media deceptions and to challenge the media for their role in fomenting divisions. They are trying to take away our history and our heritage.

Phoenix, Arizona, August 22, 2017

> If you do not tell the truth about yourself you cannot tell it about other people.
>
> Virginia Woolf

One of the things I'm going to do if I win, and I hope we do and we're certainly leading. I'm going to open up our libel laws so when they write purposely negative and horrible and false articles, we can sue them and win lots of money. We're going to open up those libel laws. So when the *New York Times* writes a hit piece which is a total disgrace or when the *Washington Post*, which is there for other reasons, writes a hit piece, we can sue them and win money instead of having no chance of winning because they're totally protected.

Campaign rally in Ft. Worth Texas, February 25, 2016

> Everyone is in favor of free speech. Hardly a day passes without its being extolled, but some people's idea of it is that they are free to say what they like, but if anyone else says anything back, that is an outrage.
>
> Winston S. Churchill

Drain the Swamp should be changed to Drain the Sewer—it's actually much worse than anyone ever thought, and it begins with the Fake News!

Tweet, July 24, 2017

> You're so full of crap, you could pass for a toilet.
>
> Kami Garcia, Beautiful Creatures

After being forced to apologize for its bad and inaccurate coverage of me after winning the election, the FAKE NEWS @nytimes is still lost!

Tweet, February 4, 2017. The New York Times *never apologized, was never "forced to apologize," because its reporting was accurate.*

> When you tear out a man's tongue, you are not proving him a liar, you're only telling the world that you fear what he might say.
>
> George R.R. Martin, *A Clash of Kings*

Little Barry Diller, who lost a fortune on Newsweek and Daily Beast, only writes badly about me. He is a sad and pathetic figure. Lives lie!

Tweet, October 10, 2015. Trump will attack newspapers, television networks and the people who run them and report on them.

> When the debate is lost slander becomes the tool of the loser.
>
> Socrates

I attack them and usually they stop attacking.

Breitbart News Sunday, May 2015. Trump seems to think his attacks on the press have slowed the press down.

> Mother Fuckers. They're going to feel pretty stupid when they find out. They're fucking with the wrong people.
>
> Robert Kirkman, *The Walking Dead*, Book Six

I have learned one thing, because I get treated very unfairly, that's what I call it, the fake media. And the fake media is not all of the media. You know they tried to say that the fake media was all the, no. The fake media is some of you. I could tell you who it is, 100 percent. Sometimes you're fake, but—but the fake media is some of the media. It bears no relationship to the truth. It's not that Fox treats me well, it's that Fox is the most accurate.

Associated Press interview, April 23, 2017

> Donald Trump is treating Fox News like it's state TV.
>
> Alex Shephard, *New Republic*

The Fake News media is officially out of control. They will do or say anything in order to get attention—never been a time like this!

Tweet, May 4, 2017

> The moment we no longer have a free press, anything can happen. What makes it possible for a totalitarian or any other dictatorship to rule is that people are not informed; how can you have an opinion if you are not informed? If everybody always lies to you, the consequence is not that you believe the lies, but rather that nobody believes anything any longer. This is because lies, by their very nature, have to be changed, and a lying government has constantly to rewrite its own history. On the receiving end you get not only one lie—a lie which you could go on for the rest of your days—but you get a great number of lies, depending on how the political wind blows. And a people that no longer can believe anything cannot make up its mind. It is deprived not only of its capacity to act but also of its capacity to think and to judge. And with such a people you can then do what you please.
>
> Hannah Arendt, during a 1974 interview with the French writer Roger Errera, republished in the *New York Review of Books*, October 28, 1978

Not only does the media give a platform to hate groups, but the media turns a blind eye to the gang violence on our streets!

Tweet, August 22, 2017, attempting to demonize the press

> Never be afraid to raise your voice for honesty and truth and compassion against injustice and lying and greed. If people all over the world . . . would do this, it would change the earth.
>
> William Faulkner

Actually, I was only kidding. You can get that baby out of here. Don't worry, I think she really believed me that I love having a baby crying while I'm speaking. That's okay. People don't understand. That's okay.

Trump expelled a mother and baby from a campaign rally, August 2, 2016.

> I love these little people; and it is not a slight thing when they, who are so fresh from God, love us.
>
> Charles Dickens

It is my opinion that many of the leaks coming out of the White House are fabricated lies made up by the #FakeNews media.

Tweet, May 23, 2017

> Group headquarters was alarmed, for there is no telling what people might find out once they felt felt free to ask whatever questions they wanted to. Colonel Cathcart sent Colonel Korn to stop it, and Colonel Korn succeeded with a rule governing the asking of questions. Colonel Korn's rule was a stroke of genius, Colonel Korn explained in his report to Colonel Cathcart. Under Colonel Korn's rule the only people permitted to ask questions were those who never did. Soon the only people attending [sessions] were those who never asked questions, and the sessions were discontinued altogether, since Clevinger, the corporal and Colonel Korn agreed that it was neither possible nor necessary to educate people who never questioned anything.
>
> Joseph Heller, *Catch-22*

I think what CNN did was unfortunate for them, as you know now they have some pretty serious problems. They have been fake news for a long time. They have been covering me in a very, very dishonest way. Do you have that also, by the way, Mr. President? With CNN and others, I mean, and others. NBC is equally as bad despite the fact that I made them a fortune with *The Apprentice*, but they forgot that. But, I will say that CNN has really taken it too seriously and I think they've hurt themselves very badly, very, very badly. And, what we want to see in the United States is honest, beautiful, free, but honest press. We want to see fair press. I think it's a very important thing. We don't want fake news. And, by the way, not everybody is fake news. But we don't want fake news. Bad thing. Very bad for our country.

At a press conference with Vladimir Putin in Poland, July 6, 2017. Putin has devoted great effort to suppressing Russia's independent press. Asking Putin if he thinks Russia's media has covered him fairly is naive and preposterous.

> The nationalistic tone of the dominant Russian media continued to drown out independent and critical journalism in 2015, stressing patriotic themes associated with Russia's 2014 military incursions into Ukraine and the launch of airstrikes in Syria in September 2015. Russian leaders and pro-government media outlets also sought to mobilize public support and suppress any dissent in the face of an economic downturn linked to falling oil prices and Ukraine-related sanctions. Deterrents to independent reporting and commentary included draconian laws and extralegal

> intimidation. Although no journalists were killed in connection with their work in 2015, the persistent threat of deadly repercussions for expressions of dissent was reinforced in February, when opposition leader Boris Nemtsov was assassinated in central Moscow.
>
> Freedomhouse, 2017

I just appreciate the meeting and I have great respect for the *New York Times*. Tremendous respect. It's very special. Always has been very special. I think I've been treated very rough. It's well out there that I've been treated extremely unfairly in a sense, in a true sense. I wouldn't only complain about the *Times*. I would say the *Times* was about the roughest of all. You could make the case the *Washington Post* was bad, but every once in awhile I'd actually get a good article. Not often, Dean, but every once in awhile.

Look, I have great respect for the *Times*, and I'd like to turn it around. I think it would make the job I am doing much easier. We're working very hard. We have great people coming in. I think you'll be very impressed with the names. We'll be announcing some very shortly.

Everybody wanted to do this. People are giving up tremendous careers in order to be subject to you folks and subject to a lot of other folks. But they're giving up a lot. I mean some are giving up tremendous businesses in order to sit for four or maybe eight or whatever the period of time is. But I think we're going to see some tremendous talent, tremendous talent coming in. We have many people for every job. I mean no matter what the job is, we have many incredible people. I think, Reince, you can sort of just confirm that. The quality of the people is very good.

The New York Times *interview, November 23, 2016, where Trump expressed his desire for the press not to be hard on him and demonstrated his misunderstanding of the press' role in America.*

> Every English poet should master the rules of grammar before he attempts to bend or break them.
>
> Robert Graves

Mexican gov doesn't want me talking about terrible border situation & horrible trade deals. Forcing Univision to get me to stop—no way!

Tweet, June 25, 2015

> Freedom of the press is not just important to democracy, it is democracy.
>
> Walter Cronkite

Based on the incredibly inaccurate coverage and reporting of the record setting Trump campaign, we are hereby revoking the press credentials of the phony and dishonest Washington Post.

Facebook post, June 13, 2016

> Don't do or say things you would not like to see on the front page of the *Washington Post*.
>
> Donald Rumsfeld

The *Times* is, it's a great, great American jewel. A world jewel.

The New York Times *interview, November 23, 2016*

> The failing @nytimes writes false story after false story about me. They don't even call to verify the facts of a story. A Fake News Joke!
>
> Tweet, June 28, 2017

"Fox and Friends'" is the most honest morning show.

Press conference, February 17, 2017

> The whole aim of practical politics is to keep the populace alarmed (and hence clamorous to be led to safety) by an endless series of hobgoblins, most of them imaginary.
>
> H.L. Mencken, *In Defense Of Women*

The @WSJ Wall Street Journal loves to write badly about me. They better be careful or I will unleash big time on them. Look forward to it.

Tweet, October 31, 2015

> The United States, almost alone today, offers the liberties and the privileges and the tools of freedom. In this land the citizens are still invited to write their plays and books, to paint their pictures, to meet for discussion, to dissent as well as to agree, to mount soapboxes in the public square, to enjoy education in all subjects without censorship, to hold court and judge one another, to compose music, to talk politics with their neighbors without wondering whether the secret police are listening, to exchange ideas as well as goods, to kid the government when it needs kidding, and to read real news of real events instead of phony

> news manufactured by a paid agent of the state. This is a fact and should give every person pause.
>
> E.B. White, *One Man's Meat*

With all of its phony unnamed sources & highly slanted & even fraudulent reporting, #Fake News is DISTORTING DEMOCRACY in our country!

Tweet, July 16, 2017

> There is a cult of ignorance in the United States, and there has always been. The strain of anti-intellectualism has been a constant thread winding its way through our political and cultural life, nurtured by the false notion that democracy means that "my ignorance is just as good as your knowledge."
>
> Isaac Asimov

Remember, don't believe "sources said" by the VERY dishonest media. If they don't name the sources, the sources don't exist.

Tweet, September 30, 2016

> President Trump on Tuesday retweeted a Fox News report citing an anonymous source that pushes back on another report that White House aide Jared Kushner tried to establish backchannel communications with Moscow.
>
> Trump's retweet comes just days after the president blasted the use of anonymous sources in news reports.
>
> The Hill, May 30, 2017

I was so happy when I heard that @Politico, one of the most dishonest political outlets, is losing a fortune. Pure scum!

Tweet, October 8, 2015

> Censorship reflects society's lack of confidence in itself. It is a hallmark of an authoritarian regime.
>
> Supreme Court Justice Potter Stewart, United States v. Ginzburg, 1965

Jerry Falwell of Liberty University was fantastic on @fox-andfriends. The Fake News should listen to what he had to say. Thanks Jerry!

Tweet, August 21, 2017. Soon after this and other recent tweets about Trump's favorite demon, the "fake news," Senate Majority Leader Mitch McConnell said, "It is my view that most news is not fake."

> Every time a newspaper dies, even a bad one, the country moves a little closer to authoritarianism.
>
> Richard Kluger

Healthcare

Donald Trump talks and tweets a lot about healthcare for one single purpose: to repeal the Affordable Care Act, also known as Obamacare.

Trump lacks vision, clarity, understanding and, most importantly, compassion about healthcare. His single-minded focus is to undo the healthcare system introduced by his predecessor, Barack Obama, whom Trump views with obsessive enmity. Trump's tweets and statements don't stray far from his July 25, 2017 remarks in Youngstown, Ohio: "Any senator who votes against repeal and replace [is] telling America they are okay with the Obamacare nightmare," and his June 15, 2015 statement, "I would do various things very quickly. I would repeal and replace the big lie, Obamacare."

Trump hasn't explained his reasons for despising Obamacare in a newspaper or magazine op-ed, in a speech devoted to healthcare, in a press conference—or anywhere. For an issue as paramount to his psyche and to the nation, the greatest depth of rationale Trump offered was at a campaign rally in Florida in October 2016: "Together we're going to deliver real change that once again puts Americans first. That begins with immediately repealing and replacing the disaster known as Obamacare. My first day in office, I am going to ask Congress to put a bill on my desk getting rid of this disastrous law and replacing it with reforms that expand choice, freedom, affordability."

Trump's heart is stone cold when it comes to the needs of actual Americans. So callous is Trump that he's willing to let Obamacare fail: "We'll let Obamacare fail, and then the Democrats are going to come to us," Trump said on July 18, 2017. For Trump, healthcare, like many other goals, is about scoring wins.

If Republican Senators are unable to pass what they are working on now, they should immediately REPEAL, and then REPLACE at a later date!

June 30, 2017, tweeting about the Senate healthcare bill. Ultimately, Trump's repeal and repeal and replace efforts failed.

> We have now just enshrined, as soon as I sign this bill, the core principle that everybody should have some basic security when it comes to their healthcare.
>
> Barack Obama

Many conversations. I just had one with a certain senator that was very convincing to that senator. So I've done a lot. I mean, last night—last night it was amazing. I was at the—you know, I was in West Virginia doing certain things and making a speech to the Boy Scouts, and that was some crowd. That was an incredible crowd.

Response to the question, "What do you think the crucial conversations [about healthcare] have been?" The Wall Street Journal interview, July 25, 2017.

> How much wood would a woodchuck chuck
> If a woodchuck could chuck wood?
> He would chuck, he would, as much as he could,
> And chuck as much wood as a woodchuck would
> If a woodchuck could chuck wood.
>
> Anonymous

Now I have to tell you, it's an unbelievably complex subject. Nobody knew that healthcare could be so complicated.

At the National Governor's Association Meeting, February 27, 2017, Washington, DC. Despite dozens of tweets about healthcare, Trump never once held a press conference, gave a speech, or wrote an article explaining his vision of healthcare.

> Being ignorant is not so much a shame, as being unwilling to learn.
>
> Benjamin Franklin

They say death, death, death. Well, Obamacare is death. That's the one that's death.

July 24, 2017

> The more a man knows, the more willing he is to learn. The less a man knows, the more positive he is that he knows everything.
>
> Robert G. Ingersoll

Unless the Republican Senators are total quitters, Repeal & Replace is not dead! Demand another vote before voting on any other bill!

Tweet, July 29, 2017, after the Republican-controlled Senate failed multiple times to repeal the Affordable Care Act.

> You can spend minutes, hours, days, weeks, or even months over-analyzing a situation; trying to put the pieces together, justifying what could've, would've happened . . . or you can just leave the pieces on the floor and move the fuck on.
>
> Tupac Shakur

If it's repeal and replace, which one do you want to go? Which form of existing conditions? I mean, there's many things.

The Wall Street Journal *interview, July 25, 2017*

> "Would you tell me, please, which way I ought to go from here?"
>
> "That depends a good deal on where you want to get to," said the Cat.
>
> "'I don't much care where,' said Alice.
>
> 'Then it doesn't matter which way you go,' said the Cat.
>
> 'So long as I get SOMEWHERE," Alice added as an explanation.

"Oh, you're sure to do that," said the Cat, "if you only walk long enough."

Lewis Carroll, Alice in Wonderland

My approach is completely different. I approach complicated problems such as how to provide healthcare for most Americans at a price we can afford the same way I solve the toughest business problems. We should hire the most knowledgeable people in the world on this subject and lock them in a room—and not unlock the door until they've agreed on the steps we need to take.

Donald Trump, Crippled America. Donald Trump's healthcare didn't happen.

> [M]illions of Americans will pay more for an insurance policy that comes with a much steeper deductible under the new Senate plan, according to some health economists and insurance experts. It could also make it much harder to find a comprehensive plan covering various conditions ranging from heart disease to depression that would not be prohibitively expensive.
>
> "This is going to be a very unstable market" where only the very sickest people resort to buying coverage on the federal exchanges at much higher prices, said Paul B. Ginsburg, a health economist and the director of the Center for Health Policy at the Brookings Institution.

> Those likely to suffer the most under the Senate plan are people who would not be eligible for any remaining subsidies, he said, because they could be priced out of the market. Most worrisome to those opposing the Senate bill is that states could give insurers leeway to offer skimpy plans that cover a lot less and exclude people with certain illnesses.
>
> *The New York Times,* June 23, 2017

People are going to have . . . they're going to have great insurance. Now, we have one more step to go. You know we have to go through the Senate and we're refining it even further. But I will tell you, Mike, I just spoke to a few of the senators and they have some great ideas also and they want to get it there.

So, the problem with Obamacare? He rushed it through, he wanted . . . although, when I say rushed it through, at the end. They were giving up everything, they were taking out everything. It wasn't a pure form of what they wanted anyway. They did the Nebraska trade where basically it was, you know, the whole thing was given away.

Look, Obamacare was a disaster. Under Obamacare, you get your doctor; that was a lie. You get your plan; that was a lie. With us, you get your doctor. You get your plan. With us you'll get hundreds and hundreds of plans. You know, one of the insurance companies, one of the big ones came to see me yesterday. They're so anxious to start going crazy and you know it's going to be like life insurance. People that buy life insurance, they're inundated with carriers. All different plans. That's what this is going to be like. And I said to them, "What do you think the good plans are going to look like?" He said, "Mr. President, we're going to have so many plans. We're going to have the low version, the high version", he used the word Cadillac. I won't tell you what car he used for the low version because I don't want you to write it because they happen to be friends of mine, you know, the head people.

The Economist *interview, May 11, 2017*

> There are some things one remembers even though they may never have happened.
>
> Harold Pinter, *Old Times*

I am not going to own it.

Talking about the failure of the Republican-controlled Senate to pass a healthcare bill. Trump will not ever take responsibility for or admit failure. That itself is a failing.

> The buck stops here.
>
> Harry S. Truman

For our neediest citizens, the Obamacare repeal and replace plan would significantly reduce the federal deficit, so it would be good for the federal government. It will cost you less money by a lot and it'll be a much better plan. You can't do better than that. When I ran for president, I made a commitment to the American people to repeal and replace Obamacare. I am pleased to report that we are very, very close to ending this health care nightmare. We are so close. The legislation working its way through Congress provides the choice and control people want the affordability they need and the quality they deserve in health care. It's a common-sense approach that restores the sacred doctor-patient relationship and you're going to finally have great healthcare at a lower price.

Paris, France, July 14, 2017. Not quite: "I am pleased to report that we are very, very close to ending this health care nightmare."

> Common sense ain't common.
>
> Will Rogers

This health care is a tough deal. I said it from the beginning. No. 1, you know, a lot of the papers were saying—actually, these guys couldn't believe it, how much I know about it. I know a lot about health care.

The New York Times *interview, July 19, 2017*

Protect me from knowing what I don't need to know. Protect me from even knowing that there are things to know that I don't know. Protect me from knowing that I decided not to know about the things that I decided not to know about. Amen.

Lord, lord, lord. Protect me from the consequences of the above prayer.

Douglas Adams, *Mostly Harmless*

Some of the Fake News Media likes to say that I am not totally engaged in healthcare. Wrong, I know the subject well & want victory for U.S.

Tweet, June 28, 2017

I like nonsense, it wakes up the brain cells. Fantasy is a necessary ingredient in living.

Dr. Seuss

Women

Where do we even begin? What words can express a normal, thinking person's outrage with Donald Trump's attitude and actions toward women?

Trump tweets thoughtful, kind words toward women, as he did during International Women's Day, "I have tremendous respect for women and the many roles they serve that are vital to the fabric of our society and our economy," and during the October 2016 presidential debate, "Nobody has more respect for women than I do. Nobody." On *Today*, Trump said, "I have tremendous respect for women, and I am going to protect women . . . [Ivanka Trump] said, 'Dad, you respect and love women so much. Could you talk about it more because people don't really understand how you feel?'"

But that's not all. After insulting and diminishing Megyn Kelly—and all women—with his infamous remark, "blood coming out of her wherever," Trump said, "I cherish women. I want to help women. I'm going to do things for women that no other candidate will be able to do."

Trump invokes his family as proof he supports women's issues and is thoughtful toward women. "I have a daughter named Ivanka and a wife named Melania who constantly want me to talk about women's health issues because they know how I feel about it. and they know how I feel about women," he said in the fall of 2015. Trump's even conjured his mother as evidence of how much he respects women. In 2016, he said, "[Ivanka and Melania said], you have such respect for women, and they say, you cherish women. You have such respect for women, you've got to speak more about it, because there's nobody that cares more for women than you. My mother was one of the great people ever in my life that I've ever met. And I have just amazing admiration and respect for women."

How much does Trump care about the women who are close to him, such as his wife? In an unscripted 1990 *Vanity Fair* interview, he said about his first wife, Ivana, "I would never buy Ivana any decent jewels or pictures. Why give her negotiable assets?"

There are plenty of adjectives to describe Donald Trump's attitude toward women, and at the top of the list, I'd put "creepy." How else do you describe somebody who walks into a women's dressing room unannounced and certainly uninvited? A Miss Teen USA contestant, who was eighteen at the time, told the CBS affiliate in Los Angeles, "Our first introduction to him was when we were at the dress rehearsal and half naked changing into our bikinis. He just came strolling right in. There was no second to put a robe on or any sort of clothing or anything. Some girls were topless. Other girls were naked." Trump doesn't deny he did this. In fact, he wears this outrage like a medal: "I'll go backstage before a show, and everyone's getting dressed and ready and everything else," Trump told Howard Stern in 2005.

In the 1990s, Trump joked about dating underage girls: "I'm going to be dating her in ten years, can you believe it?" he said about a pre-teen, around ten years old. Trump was forty-six years old at the time.

As president, Trump's been able to put his caring but not caring about women philosophy into action.

In April 2017, Trump signed a bill to cut all federal funding to Planned Parenthood. Trump signed an executive order rescinding the Fair Pay and Safe Workplaces Executive Order, and by doing so, made it easier for federal contractors with a history of sex discrimination to get contracts. These are just two of the numerous actions that Trump has taken since assuming the presidency that hurt women.

Trump's appointing Neil Gorsuch to the Supreme Court puts a woman's right to choose what to do with her body one vote closer to being overturned.

Trump's proposed budget cuts numerous programs that help many poor and rural women.

In August 2017, Trump cut funding for teen pregnancy programs.

It's as if Trump is on a crusade *against* women.

You know, it doesn't really matter what [they] write as long as you've got a young and beautiful piece of ass.

1991, quoted in Esquire *magazine*

The beauty of a woman is not in a facial mode but the true beauty in a woman is reflected in her soul. It is the caring that she lovingly gives the passion that she shows. The beauty of a woman grows with the passing years.

Audrey Hepburn

We may live in houses in the suburbs but our minds and emotions are still only a short step out of the jungle. In primitive times, women clung to the strongest males for protection. High-status males displayed their prowess through their kick-ass attitudes. They did not give a crap about what other people in the tribe thought. That kind of attitude was and still is associated with the kind of men women find attractive. It may not be politically correct to say but who cares. It is common sense and it's true—and always will be.

Think Big, *2008*

The day will come when men will recognize woman as his peer, not only at the fireside, but in councils of the nation. Then, and not until then, will there be the perfect comradeship, the ideal union between the sexes that shall result in the highest development of the race.

Susan B. Anthony

I'm automatically attracted to beautiful—I just start kissing them. It's like a magnet. Just kiss. I don't even wait. And when you're a star, they let you do it. You can do anything. . . . Grab 'em by the pussy. You can do anything.

Trump during a conversation with Billy Bush, then the host of "Access Hollywood." Trump's now-infamous comment, "Grab 'em by the pussy," was dismissed by his supporters as "locker room talk." Many pro athletes emphasized that that's not how they talk in the locker room. The counter tweets were overwhelming. Kendall Marshall: "PSA: sexual advances without consent is NOT locker room talk." Robbie Rogers: "I'm offended as an athlete that @realDonaldTrump keeps using this "locker room talk" as an excuse." Dahntay Jones: "Claiming Trump's comments are "locker room banter" is to suggest they are somehow acceptable. They aren't."

I love to see a young girl go out and grab the world by the lapels. Life's a bitch. You've got to go out and kick ass.

Maya Angelou

As far as Planned Parenthood is concerned, I'm pro-life. I'm totally against abortion, having to do with Planned Parenthood. But millions and millions of women—cervical cancer, breast cancer—are helped by Planned Parenthood. So you can say whatever you want, but they have millions of women going through Planned Parenthood that are helped greatly. And I wouldn't fund it. I would defund it because of the abortion factor, which they say is 3 percent. I don't know what percentage it is. They say it's 3 percent. But I would defund it, because I'm pro-life. But millions of women are helped by Planned Parenthood.

Republican debate, Feb 25, 2016

> If I had a world of my own, everything would be nonsense. Nothing would be what it is, because everything would be what it isn't. And contrary wise, what is, it wouldn't be. And what it wouldn't be, it would. You see?
>
> Lewis Carroll, *Alice's Adventures in Wonderland*

You have to treat 'em like shit.

New York Magazine, *November 9, 1992, talking about how to treat women.*

> Of all the evils for which man has made himself responsible, none is so degrading, so shocking or

so brutal as his abuse of the better half of humanity; the female sex.

Mahatma Gandhi

Nobody cares about the talent. There's only one talent you care about, and that's the look talent. You don't give a shit if a girl can play a violin like the greatest violinist in the world. You want to know what does she look like.

On beauty and beauty pageants, quoted in TrumpNation

No matter how plain a woman may be, if truth and honesty are written across her face, she will be beautiful.

Eleanor Roosevelt

You're in such good shape. She's in such good physical shape. Beautiful.

Remarks made about Brigitte Macron, France's First Lady, July 2017. In one sentence, Trump both insulted the wife of the French president and hit on her. Brigitte Macron is sixty-four years old.

> A really strong woman accepts the war she went through and is ennobled by her scars.
>
> Carly Simon

I love women. They've come into my life. They've gone out of my life. Even those who have exited somewhat ungracefully still have a place in my heart. I only have one regret in the women department—that I never had the opportunity to court Lady Diana Spencer. I met her on a number of occasions.

In his 1997 book, Trump: The Art of the Comeback

> Let's be very clear: Strong men—men who are truly role models—don't need to put down women to make themselves feel powerful. People who are truly strong lift others up. People who are truly powerful bring others together.
>
> Michelle Obama

Heidi Klum. Sadly, she's no longer a 10.

Commenting on supermodel Heidi Klum turning forty-two years old.

> The Presidency . . . is pre-eminently a place of moral leadership.
>
> Franklin D. Roosevelt

Women have one of the great acts of all time. The smart ones act very feminine and needy, but inside they are real killers. The person who came up with the expression "the weaker sex" was either very naive or had to be kidding. I have seen women manipulate men with just a twitch of their eye—or perhaps another body part.

Trump: The Art of the Comeback

> Behind every great man is a woman rolling her eyes.
>
> Jim Carrey

I am going to be dating her in 10 years. Can you believe it?

Commenting on a ten-year-old girl who caught Trump's eye, overheard on an Entertainment Tonight *video, 1992.*

> Lolita, light of my life, fire of my loins. My sin, my soul. Lo-lee-ta: the tip of the tongue taking a trip of three steps down the palate to tap, at three, on

the teeth. Lo. Lee. Ta. She was Lo, plain Lo, in the morning, standing four feet ten in one sock. She was Lola in slacks. She was Dolly at school. She was Dolores on the dotted line. But in my arms she was always Lolita. Did she have a precursor? She did, indeed she did. In point of fact, there might have been no Lolita at all had I not loved, one summer, an initial girl-child. In a princedom by the sea. Oh when? About as many years before Lolita was born as my age was that summer.

Vladimir Nabokov, *Lolita*

You know who's our primary representative [in Japan] now? Caroline Kennedy. You know how she got the job? She went to the White House, she said, "I'd love to have a job. I have nothing to do." They said, "How would you like to be the ambassador to Japan?" She goes, "Really?" And [Japan's Prime Minister] Abe, who's a killer—he's great, he's already knocking the hell out of the yen—and he's wining and dining her. I watch him all the time wining and dining. Just doing a number on her.

Campaign rally, Phoenix, Arizona, July 11, 2015.

Women are the largest untapped reservoir of talent in the world.

Hillary Clinton

You're disgusting.

Words said during a deposition to a female lawyer who asked to take a break to breastfeed her child.

> A pair of substantial mammary glands have the advantage over the two hemispheres of the most learned professor's brain in the art of compounding a nutritive fluid for infants.
>
> Oliver Wendell Holmes

No one has more respect for women than Donald Trump.

Presidential debate, October 2016

> Above all, don't lie to yourself. The man who lies to himself and listens to his own lie comes to a point that he cannot distinguish the truth within him, or around him, and so loses all respect for himself and for others. And having no respect he ceases to love.
>
> Fyodor Dostoevsky

I cherish women. I want to help women. I'm going to be able to do things for women that no other candidate would be able to do.

August 2015

> There are only three things to be done with a woman. You can love her, suffer for her, or turn her into literature.
>
> Henry Miller

I don't think Ivanka would do that inside the magazine. Although she does have a very nice figure. I've said that if Ivanka weren't my daughter, perhaps I would be dating her.

On The View *in 2006, answering a question about whether his daughter, Ivanka, would pose nude,* Playboy Magazine *interview.*

> I know it when I see it.
>
> Supreme Court Justice Potter Stewart writing about pornography in *Jacobellis v. Ohio*, 1964

Such a nasty woman.

Spoken about Hillary Clinton, presidential debate, October 19, 2016.

> Sometimes you have to be a bitch to get things done.
>
> Madonna

All of the women on *The Apprentice* flirted with me, consciously or unconsciously. That's to be expected.

Trump, How to Get Rich

> In my opinion, we don't devote nearly enough scientific research to finding a cure for jerks.
>
> Bill Watterson

I like the way she used to look. I don't like the way she looks now. . . . She's a solid four. She was an eight, she wasn't a 10. She went from being very flat-chested. I view that a person who is flat-chested is very hard to be a 10. It has been extraordinary, you have to have the face of

Vivian Leigh to be a 10 if you are flat-chested. She went from an eight to a solid four.

Talking about Nicolette Sheridan, an actor on Desperate Housewives, *Howard Stern Show, 2005*

> Some people think having large breasts makes a woman stupid. Actually, it's quite the opposite: A woman having large breasts makes men stupid.
>
> Rita Rudner

There's a lot of women out there that demand that the husband act like the wife and you know there's a lot of husbands that listen to that. So you know, they go for it.

A 2005 radio interview explaining why he doesn't change diapers.

> Real fatherhood means love and commitment and sacrifice and a willingness to share responsibility and not walking away from one's children.
>
> William Bennett

I would like to think she would find another career or find another company if that was the case.

Answering a question from a reporter about what he'd tell his daughter, Ivanka, to do if she were sexually harassed at work, August 1, 2016.

> I am hopeful that others who have suffered sexual harassment will not become discouraged by my experience, but instead will find the strength to speak out about this serious problem.
>
> Anita Hill

The answer is that there has to be some form of punishment. For the woman.

During a town hall meeting in Green Bay, Wisconsin, during which Chris Matthews asked Trump if thought women who had an abortion should be punished, March 30, 2016.

> What was this power, this insidious threat, this invisible gun to her head that controlled her life . . . this terror of being called names?
>
> She had stayed a virgin so she wouldn't be called a tramp or a slut; had married so she wouldn't be called an old maid; faked orgasms so she wouldn't be called frigid; had children so she wouldn't be called barren; had not been a feminist because she

> didn't want to be called queer and a man hater; never nagged or raised her voice so she wouldn't be called a bitch . . .
>
> She had done all that and yet, still, this stranger had dragged her into the gutter with the names that men call women when they are angry.
>
> Fannie Flagg, *Fried Green Tomatoes at the Whistle Stop Cafe*

I'm pro-life, but I changed my view a number of years ago. One of the primary reasons I changed [was] a friend of mine's wife was pregnant, and he didn't really want the baby. He was crying as he was telling me the story. He ends up having the baby and the baby is the apple of his eye. It's the greatest thing that's ever happened to him. And you know here's a baby that wasn't going to be let into life. And I heard this, and some other stories, and I am pro-life.

Interview with Christian Broadcasting Network, April 2011

> But the preservation of life seems to be rather a slogan than a genuine goal of the anti-abortion forces; what they want is control. Control over behavior: power over women. Women in the anti-choice movement want to share in male power over women, and do so by denying their own womanhood, their own rights and responsibilities.

> We are not going back to the Dark Ages. We are not going to let anybody in this country have that kind of power over any girl or woman. There are great powers, outside the government and in it, trying to legislate the return of darkness. We are not great powers. But we are the light. Nobody can put us out.
>
> Ursula K. Le Guin, "The Princess," January 1982

What surprises many people is that beautiful women love me. For the first season of *The Apprentice,* one broadcast exec said, "To be successful, large numbers of women would have to watch, and why would women want to watch Donald Trump?" I said, "I have not done so badly with women." As it turned out, the biggest audience for The Apprentice by far is women.

Think Big, *2008*

> And I realized that I'd tolerated him this long because of self-doubt.
>
> Anne Rice, *Interview with the Vampire*

As far as Planned Parenthood is concerned, I'm pro-life. I'm totally against abortion, having to do with Planned Parenthood. But millions and millions of women—cervical cancer, breast cancer—are helped by Planned Parenthood. So you can say whatever you want, but they have millions of women going through Planned Parenthood that are helped greatly. And I wouldn't fund it. I would defund it because of the abortion factor, which they say is 3%. I don't know what percentage it is. They say it's 3%. But I would defund it, because I'm pro-life. But millions of women are helped by Planned Parenthood.

Republican debate, February 2016

> Anyone can speak Troll. All you have to do is point and grunt.
>
> J.K. Rowling, *Harry Potter and the Goblet of Fire*

Take a look. Look at her. Look at her words. And you tell me what you think. I don't think so.

Talking about Natasha Stoynoff, a former People magazine reporter who accused Trump of sexual assault, during a rally in West Palm Beach, Florida, October 14, 2016. Trump's point that Ms. Stoynoff wasn't pretty enough for him to want to sleep with was as obvious as the noonday sun in August.

> Most women are all too familiar with men like Calvin Smith. Men whose sense of prerogative renders them deaf when women say, "No thanks," "Not interested," or even "Fuck off, creep."
>
> Jon Krakauer, Missoula: Rape and the Justice System in a College Town

I've always had a great relationship to the women I work with. The relationship has been amazing in terms of thousands of employees, top-level employees. And, you know, I was one of the first people in the construction industry to put women in charge of major construction projects and my relationship has been great. I have many executives that are women and doing a phenomenal job. And I'm doing very well with the women voters. So I don't really worry about those false accusations.

Answering a question about his treatment of Megyn Kelly and Carly Fiorina, ABC This Week *interview, Aug 9, 2015*

> You painted a naked woman because you enjoyed looking at her, put a mirror in her hand and you called the painting "Vanity," thus morally condemning the woman whose nakedness you had depicted for you own pleasure.
>
> John Berger, *Ways of Seeing*

I don't know why, but I seem to bring out either the best or worst in women. Even Katarina Witt, the great Olympic figure-skating champion, caused me some angst. Because I built and ran the Wollman Skating Rink in Central Park, I became something of a factor in the ice-skating business. One day I received a phone call from Katarina asking if she could come to my office to say hello. Everything went well; Katarina invited me to see her opening-night performance at Madison Square Garden.

Katarina asked me what I thought of the evening. I told her that, while I liked her skating, I thought the music she skated to was horrible. "I know you want to be artistic," I said, "but you really ought to choose music that's more mainstream, something people will enjoy." Katarina was not pleased with my comments and I could see at a glance that steely German temperament.

After that, every article written about Katarina Witt included claims that I had asked her out and she had turned me down.

The Art of the Comeback, *1997*

> If you do not tell the truth about yourself you cannot tell it about other people.
>
> Virginia Woolf

I've always been good to women and there will be nobody better to women as a president, because I'll take care—when I talk about health issues, I will take care of women like nobody else can. I will be so good to women. I cherish women. I will be so good to women. I will work hard to protect women.

CNN interview with Chris Cuomo, August 11, 2015. On April 13, 2017 Trumped signed a bill whose objective is to cut off federal funding for Planned Parenthood, The law, according to The New York Times, *"nullifies a rule completed in the last days of the Obama administration that effectively barred state and local governments from withholding federal funding for family planning services related to contraception, sexually transmitted infections, fertility, pregnancy care, and breast and cervical cancer screening from qualified health providers—regardless of whether they also performed abortions."*

> "Actually," said Jace, "I prefer to think that I'm a liar in a way that's uniquely my own."
>
> Cassandra Clare, *City of Ashes*

Words and Language

Few presidents have been as eloquent as Thomas Jefferson, Abraham Lincoln, John F. Kennedy, or Barack Obama. It's a gift, a rare gift. Other presidents, even though they may have lacked a golden linguistic core, spoke clearly and precisely. Most presidents have been able to carry their train of thought from the sentence's beginning to the period at the end of the sentence.

But not Donald Trump.

Trump does not speak in sentences. That's not a condescending, gratuitous insult; it's how he often speaks. Trump and English grammar are like the same magnetic pole, repelling each other the closer they get. Trump and English grammar are like matter and antimatter, mutually annihilating each other if they are in the same place at the same time. What's the right word to describe Trump's brand of English—different? complicated? knotty?

hazardous? Whichever word best describes how Trump talks, his speech and tweets make translators tear their hair out because Trump can't be translated into other languages. I mean that literally. Translation requires coherence. You can't translate rambling words, strung together by threads blown by gale force winds. South Korean television and newspapers, for example, often don't even try to translate Trump's tweets into Korean; they just publish his tweets as is, in Trumplish.

The adjective that best describes Trump's brand of English is incoherent.

Incoherent.

One Japanese translator described the Trump translation problem this way to *The Guardian*[1]:

> *"[W]hen the logic is not clear or a sentence is just left hanging in the air, then we have a problem. We try to grasp the context and get at the core message, but in Trump's case, it's so incoherent. You're interpreting, and then suddenly the sentence stops making sense, and we risk ending up sounding stupid.*
>
> *There's no way we can explain what he really means on air, so we just try to do our best. Japanese viewers are probably getting used to his idiosyncrasies by now."*

It's not much easier for native English speakers, either. It's one thing to try to divine the meaning inside ancient religious scrolls written millennia ago, but it's another when few people understand what the President of the

1. https://www.theguardian.com/us-news/2017/jun/06/trump-translation-interpreters

United States is thinking. Trump babbles and rambles nearly every time he says something.

During an interview with the *Associated Press*, Trump said:

I saved $725 million on the 90 planes. Just 90. Now there are 3,000 planes that are going to be ordered. On 90 planes I saved $725 million. It's actually a little bit more than that, but it's $725 million. General Mattis, who had to sign the deal when it came to his office, said, "I've never seen anything like this in my life." We went from a company that wanted more money for the planes to a company that cut. And the reason they cut—same planes, same everything—was because of me. I mean, because that's what I do.

During one of the Republican debates, Trump babbled:

I'm just saying very simply we have a country that I've never seen anything like it. I've been going over budgets and looking at budgets. We don't bid things out. We don't bid out, as an example, the drug industry, pharmaceutical industry. They don't go out to bid. They just pay almost as if you walk into a drugstore. That's what they're paying.

I'm self-funding my campaign. Nobody is going to be taking care of me. I don't want anybody's money. I will tell you something. We're going to go out to bid in virtually every different facet of our government. We're going to save a fortune.

Speech follows thought. In Trump's case, both are incoherent, rambling, and disorganized. That's a great danger for America and the world because clarity of thought is one of a president's most important assets—or should be.

It's not my place to offer Donald Trump advice, but I'm going give it. Tweet what you want because nobody expects eloquence and subtlety in 140 characters. When giving interviews, stick to one-sentence answers. And for God's sake, when giving speeches that your speechwriters have written, stick to the script.

One other piece of advice. Read books. It's not too late to absorb good writing, good grammar, and clarity of thought.

Despite the constant negative press covfefe.

Tweet, May 31, 2017. Trump, it seems, fell asleep mid-tweet. He was probably writing, "Despite the negative press coverage," but no matter, "covfefe" instantly became a meme, a new dictionary listing, and t-shirt slogan. Then-press secretary Sean Spicer told reporters, "The President and a small group know exactly what he meant."

Twas brillig, and the slithy toves
  Did gyre and gimble in the wabe:
All mimsy were the borogoves,
  And the mome raths outgrabe.

Lewis Carroll, "Jabberwocky," 1872

I don't really know. . . . But in that time. And don't forget, Crimea was given away during Obama. Not during Trump. In fact, I was on one of the shows, I said they're exactly right, they didn't have it as it exactly. But he was—this—Crimea was gone during the Obama administration, and he gave, he allowed it to get away. You know, he can talk tough all he wants, in the meantime he talked tough to North Korea. And he didn't actually. He didn't talk tough to North Korea. You know, we have a big problem with North Korea. Big. Big, big. You look at all of the things, you look at the line in the sand. The red line in the sand in Syria. He didn't do the shot. I did the shot. Had he done that shot, he wouldn't have had—had he done something dramatic, because if you remember, they had a tremendous gas attack after he made that statement. Much bigger than the one they had with me.

The New York Times *interview, July 2017, in response to a question about Crimea, Hillary Clinton, and Russian sanctions. Good luck trying to understand what Trump is saying or thinking.*

> One of the Georges—I forget which—once said that a certain number of hours' sleep each night—I cannot recall at the moment how many—made a man something which for the time being has slipped my memory.
>
> P.G. Wodehouse, *Mike and Psmith*

Our country has been divided for decade. Sometimes you need protest in order to heel, & we will heel, & be stronger than ever before.

Tweet, August 20, 2017. Trump deleted this tweet and replaced it with a correctly spelled one. On September 1, Trump again tweeted using the word "heel," when he meant "heal": "Texas is heeling fast thanks to all of the great men & women who have been working so hard. But still, so much to do. Will be back tomorrow!" *He repealed and replaced that tweet, too.*

> If a word in the dictionary were misspelled, how would we know?
>
> Steven Wright

Well, first of all, I want you to understand that the Democrats, and I've watched them very intensely, even though it's a very, very boring thing to watch, that the Democrats are doing nothing with Social Security. They're leaving it the way it is. In fact, they want to increase it. They want to actually give more.

And that's what we're up against. And whether we like it or not, that is what we're up against.

I will do everything within my power not to touch Social Security, to leave it the way it is; to make this country rich again; to bring back our jobs; to get rid of deficits; to get rid of waste, fraud and abuse, which is rampant in this country, rampant, totally rampant.

Trump's answer to the question during the final GOP debate, "Mr. Trump, you don't want to raise the retirement age, and you also don't want to cut benefits, even for wealthier Americans. But according to the Social Security Administration, unless adjustments are made, Social Security is projected to run out of money within 20 years. So specifically, what would you do to stop that from happening?"

> Grammar is a piano I play by ear. All I know about grammar is its power.
>
> Joan Didion

But things change. There has to be flexibility. Let me give you an example. President Xi, we have a, like, a really great relationship. For me to call him a currency manipulator and then say, "By the way, I'd like you to solve the North Korean problem," doesn't work. So you have to have a certain flexibility, Number One. Number Two, from the time I took office till now, you know, it's a very exact thing. It's not like generalities.

Associated Press interview, April 2017

> "Just because you're sober, don't think you're a good driver, Cookie."
>
> John Irving, *Last Night in Twisted River*

But President Xi, from the time I took office, he has not, they have not been currency manipulators. Because there's a certain respect because he knew I would do something or whatever. But more importantly than him not being a currency manipulator the bigger picture, bigger than even currency manipulation, if he's helping us with North Korea, with nuclear and all of the things that go along with it, who would call, what am I going to do, say, "By the way, would you help us with North Korea? And also, you're a currency manipulator." It doesn't work that way.... And the media, some of them get it, in all fairness. But you know some of them either don't get it, in which case they're very stupid people, or they just don't want to say it. You know because of a couple of them said, "He didn't call them a currency manipulator." Well, for two reasons. Number One, he's not, since my time. You know, very specific formula. You would think it's like generalities, it's not. They have—they've actually—their currency's gone up. So it's a very, very specific formula. And I said, "How badly have they been." They said, "Since you got to office they have not manipulated their currency." That's Number One, but much more important, they are working with us on North Korea. Now maybe that'll work out or maybe it won't. Can you imagine?

Associated Press interview, April 2017

> Sneak into my theater will you, you wasically wabbit?
>
> Elmer Fudd, "Box-Office Bunny," 1990

I will know more about the problems of this world by the time I sit, and you look at what's going in this world right now by people that supposedly know, this world is a mess.

Republican debate, September 16, 2015

> Vowels were something else. He didn't like them and they didn't like him. There were only five of them, but they seemed to be everywhere. Why, you could go through twenty words without bumping into some of the shyer consonants, but it seemed as if you couldn't tiptoe past a syllable without waking up a vowel. Consonants, you know pretty much where you stood, but you could never trust a vowel.
>
> Jerry Spinelli, *Maniac Magee*

I want to achieve growth. We're the highest-taxed nation in the world, essentially, you know, of the size. But we're the highest-taxed nation in the world. We have—nobody knows what the number is. I mean, it used to be, when we talked during the debate, $2.5 trillion, right, when the most elegant person—right? I call him Mr. Elegant. I mean, that was a great debate. We did such a great job. But at that time I was talking $2.5 trillion. I guess it's $5 trillion now. Whatever it is, it's a lot more. So we have anywhere from 4 [trillion] to 5 or even more trillions of dollars sitting offshore.

Trump's rambling answer to the question during a Wall Street Journal *interview, "Can you tell us what you—you know, what you want to achieve fundamentally in tax reform?" July 25, 2017*

> It's funny. All you have to do is say something nobody understands and they'll do practically anything you want them to.
>
> J.D. Salinger, *The Catcher in the Rye*

Some of you here tonight might even have camped out in this yard when Mike [Pence] was the governor of Indiana, but the scouting was very, very important.

Speech at Boy Scout Jamboree, Glen Jean, West Virginia, July 24, 2017

> Writing is thinking. To write well is to think clearly. That's why it's so hard.
>
> David McCullough

Oh, you're Boy Scouts, but you know life. You know life. So—look at you.

Speech at Boy Scout Jamboree, Glen Jean, West Virginia July 24, 2017

> Clear thinking becomes clear writing; one can't exist without the other.
>
> William Zinsser

I have learned one thing, because I get treated very unfairly, that's what I call it, the fake media. And the fake media is not all of the media. You know they tried to say that the fake media was all the, no. The fake media is some of you. I could tell you who it is, one hundred percent. Sometimes you're fake, but—but the fake media is some of the media. It bears no relationship to the truth. It's not that Fox treats me well, it's that Fox is the most accurate.

Associated Press interview, April 2017

> Couric: And when it comes to establishing your world view, I was curious, what newspapers and magazines did you regularly read before you were tapped for this—to stay informed and to understand the world?
>
> Palin: I've read most of them again with a great appreciation for the press, for the media—

Couric: But what ones specifically? I'm curious.

Palin: Um, all of them, any of them that have been in front of me over all these years.

Couric: Can you name any of them?

Palin: I have a vast variety of sources where we get our news.

From Katie Couric's interview with Sarah Palin candidate for Vice President, 2008

I will stop Iran from getting nuclear weapons. And we won't be using a man like Secretary Kerry that has absolutely no concept of negotiation, who's making a horrible and laughable deal, who's just being tapped along as they make weapons right now, and then goes into a bicycle race at 72 years old, and falls and breaks his leg. I won't be doing that. And I promise I will never be in a bicycle race. That I can tell you.

From Trump's speech announcing his candidacy for president, June 16, 2015. From Iran's nuclear weapons to a bicycle accident in a single thought.

Forgive me my nonsense as I also forgive the nonsense of those who think they talk sense.

Robert Frost

My son is a high-quality person.

July 12, 2017, after the revelation that Donald Trump Jr. met with a Russian to obtain information to influence the 2016 presidential election. "High-quality" is a word used to describe a toaster or shaving cream, not a word that a father uses to talk about his children.

> Quality means doing it right when no one is looking.
>
> Henry Ford

Look, I'm just saying very simply we have a country that I've never seen anything like it. I've been going over budgets and looking at budgets. We don't bid things out. We don't bid out, as an example, the drug industry, pharmaceutical industry. They don't go out to bid. They just pay almost as if you walk into a drugstore. That's what they're paying.

I'm self-funding my campaign. Nobody is going to be taking care of me. I don't want anybody's money. I will tell you something. We're going to go out to bid in virtually every different facet of our government. We're going to save a fortune.

Talking about how he'd balance the budget, GOP debate, 2016.

> It's perfectly obvious that there is some genetic factor that distinguishes humans from other animals and that it is language-specific. The theory of that genetic component, whatever it turns out to be, is what is called universal grammar.
>
> Noam Chomsky

When I did this now I said, I probably, maybe will confuse people, maybe I'll expand that, you know, lengthen the time because it should be over with, in my opinion, should have been over with a long time ago.

From a conversation with Lester Holt on NBC, February 2017.

> Don't gobblefunk around with words.
>
> Roald Dahl, The BFG

There is no collusion between certainly myself and my campaign, but I can always speak for myself—and the Russians, zero.

Speaking at a joint press conference with Colombian president, Juan Manuel Santos, May 19, 2017

Everybody thinks I'm crazy.
Yesiree, that's me, that's me.
That's what I'm cracked up to be.
I chop a hole in every tree.
Knock on wood.
Well, knock on wood.
So, I'm crazy, so what?
What can I do?
So are you!

Woody Woodpecker, 1941

Number One, there's great responsibility. When it came time to, as an example, send out the 59 missiles, the Tomahawks in Syria. I'm saying to myself, "You know, this is more than just like, 79 (*sic*) missiles. This is death that's involved," because people could have been killed. This is risk that's involved, because if the missile goes off and goes in a city or goes in a civilian area—you know, the boats were hundreds of miles away—and if this missile goes off and lands in the middle of a town or a hamlet . . . every decision is much harder than you'd normally make. (Unintelligible). . . . This is involving death and life and so many things . . . So it's far more responsibility. (Unintelligible). . . . The financial cost of everything is so massive, every agency. This is thousands of times bigger, the United States, than the biggest company in the world. The second-largest company in the world is the Defense Department. The third-largest company in the world is Social Security. The fourth-largest—you know, you go down the list. . . . It's massive. And every agency is, like, bigger than any company. So you know, I really just see the bigness of it all, but also the responsibility. And the human responsibility. You know, the human life that's involved in some of the decisions.

Associated Press interview, April 2017, in response to question about the responsibility of being president.

> Fayvrrtep fitsenge lu kxanì. Fìpoti oel tspìyang, fte tìkenong liyevu aylaru.
>
> These demons are forbidden here. I will kill this one as a lesson to the others.
>
> Quotation from a Na'vi from James Cameron's 2009 movie, *Avatar*. The Na'vi language is a made-up language, like English seems to be for some people.

In fact, they also did. I never thought I had the ability to not watch. Like, people think I watch MSNBC's] *Morning Joe*. I don't watch *Morning Joe*. I never thought I had the ability to, and who used to treat me great by the way, when I played the game. I never thought I had the ability to not watch what is unpleasant, if it's about me. Or pleasant. But when I see it's such false reporting and such bad reporting and false reporting that I've developed an ability that I never thought I had. I don't watch things that are unpleasant. I just don't watch them.

Associated Press interview, April 2017

> Sponges grow in the ocean. That just kills me. I wonder how much deeper the ocean would be if that didn't happen.
>
> Steven Wright

We'll do some questions, unless you have enough questions.

Press conference, February 2017

> Some people have a way with words, and other people . . . oh, uh, not have way.
>
> Steve Martin

People want the border wall. My base definitely wants the border wall, my base really wants it—you've been to many of the rallies. Okay, the thing they want more than anything is the wall. My base, which is a big base; I think my base is 45 percent. You know, it's funny. The Democrats, they have a big advantage in the Electoral College. Big,

big, big advantage. . . . The Electoral College is very difficult for a Republican to win, and I will tell you, the people want to see it. They want to see the wall.

Associated Press interview, April 23, 2017

> There is no confusion like the confusion of a simple mind.
>
> F. Scott Fitzgerald

After 200 days, rarely has any Administration achieved what we have achieved..not even close! Don't believe the Fake News Suppression Polls!

Tweet, August 9, 2017

> In a fascist system, it's not the lies that count but the muddying. When citizens can't tell real news from fake, they give up their demands for accountability bit by bit.
>
> Naomi Wolf

The Military

Trump has assumed the role of America's Commander in Chief with naivety, hubris, and disdain. During the campaign, Trump said, "Under the leadership of Barack Obama and Hillary Clinton, I think the generals have been reduced to rubble. They have been reduced to a point where it's embarrassing to our country." At another presidential campaign event, Trump proclaimed, "I know more about ISIS than the generals do, believe me. I would bomb the shit out of them."

If one had hoped that Trump would sober up and become informed, or even wise, after he sat in the Oval Office—as if the spirits of Lincoln, Truman and Kennedy filled him—one was bound to be disappointed. On August 2, 2017, Senator Lindsay Graham reported a conversation he had President Trump: "If there's going to be a war to stop [President Kim Jong Un], it will be over there. If thousands die, they're going to die over there. They're not going to die here. And [Trump] told me that to my face. . . . There is a military option to destroy North Korea's program and North Korea itself." Contrast that with Trump's intellectually stunted August 1, 2017 explanation of how he'll deal with North Korea. Speaking after his first full Cabinet meeting, Trump said, "We will handle North Korea. We are gonna be able to handle them. It will be handled. We handle everything." Trump does not inspire confidence as the leader of the most powerful military in the world.

Trump zigzags between incoherent and vague to bombastic and scary. On August 9, 2017, Trump said, "North Korea best not make any more threats to the United States. They will be met with fire and fury like the world has never seen. . . . [Kim Jong-Un] has been very threatening beyond a normal state. They will be met with fire, fury and frankly power the likes of which this world has never seen before." Trump's statement drove Asian stock markets down and antacid sales up.

Trump doesn't understand the military. That was clear from an NBC report on August 2, 2017 about Trump using an analogy about the renovation of the 21 Club in New York in the 1980s to explain why, in his view, America was losing the war in Afghanistan. NBC reported:

> *Trump told his advisers that the restaurant, Manhattan's elite '21' Club, had shut its doors for a year and hired an expensive consultant to craft a plan for a renovation. After a year, Trump said, the consultant's only suggestion was that the restaurant needed a bigger kitchen.*
>
> *Officials said Trump kept stressing the idea that lousy advice cost the owner a year of lost business and that talking*

to the restaurant's waiters instead might have yielded a better result. He also said the tendency is to assume if someone isn't a three-star general he doesn't know what he's talking about, and that in his own experience in business talking to low-ranking workers has gotten him better outcomes.

Trump not only used an odd metaphor to talk about war, but he was wrong on the facts, too. The restaurant renovated a sixty-year-old kitchen, a job that took six months.

In April 2017, Trump said this when talking about the 21,000 pound bomb dropped on an ISIS tunnel complex in Afghanistan: "Everybody knows exactly what happened. What I do is I authorize my military." *My military*. Trump is wrong. The military belongs to America; it's not the president's private army.

In July 2017, Trump tweeted a ban on transgender Americans serving in the military. (There's doubt that this ban will ever become policy; as of this book's publication, it has not.) Trump's proclamation (which he claimed, without evidence, was formulated in "consultation with my Generals and military experts") is likely to have a detrimental effect on the U.S. military by depriving the armed forces of patriotic, intelligent personnel.

The military under Trump is in for rocky times. But America is stronger than Trump is conniving and foolish.

26,000 unreported sexual assaults in the military-only 238 convictions. What did these geniuses expect when they put men & women together?

Tweet, May 8, 2013

> Women have to work much harder to make it in this world. It really pisses me off that women don't get the same opportunities as men do, or money for that matter. Because let's face it, money gives men the power to run the show. It gives men the power to define our values and to define what's sexy and what's feminine and that's bullshit. At the end of the day, it's not about equal rights, it's about how we think. We have to reshape our own perception of how we view ourselves.
>
> Beyoncé

The F-35 fighter jet—I saved—I got involved in the negotiation. It's 2,500 jets. I negotiated for 90 planes, got 10. I got $725 million off the price.

May 1, 2017. The New York Times *reported that most of the price negotiation was done during the Obama administration.*

> You can spend your whole life building a wall of facts between you and anything real.
>
> Chuck Palahniuk

You have arms and legs and everything else laying all over the town where it is. A real problem too. But you know, it just seemed, when they start using gases, it's something that is just terrible. But honestly barrel bombs are incredible when you see the damage done by these. . . .

My friend said to me that, he said you know it's interesting, he said you hit them because of the gases but the barrel bombs are worse. He said what they do to people is unbelievable. You have arms and legs laying two hundred yards away.

And despite that there was something about the gases. It's just terrible. And I guess it was also that he violated the deal that was done with Obama. He's got gas all over the place. He's got gas all over the place.

Time *magazine interview, May 11, 2017*

> A man's grammar, like Caesar's wife, should not only be pure, but above suspicion of impurity.
>
> Edgar Allan Poe

My original instinct was to pull out. And historically, I like following my instincts.

But all my life I've heard that decisions are much different when you sit behind the desk in the Oval Office, in other words, when you're president of the United States.

So I studied Afghanistan in great detail and from every conceivable angle.

Speech about America's next steps in Afghanistan, August 22, 2017. A New York Times *editorial headline described Trump's vision for Afghanistan this way: "Mr. Trump on Afghanistan: More of the Same; No End in Sight."*

> In their huge bedroom that night, Tyr said to Thor, "I hope you know what you are doing."
>
> "Of course I do," said Thor. But he didn't. He was just doing whatever he felt like doing. That was what Thor did best.
>
> Neil Gaiman, *Norse Mythology*

Well, Napoleon finished a little bit bad. But I asked that. So I asked the president, so what about Napoleon? [President Macron of France] said: "No, no, no. What he did was incredible. He designed Paris." [garbled] The street grid, the way they work, you know, the spokes. He did so many things even beyond. And his one problem is he didn't go to Russia that night because he had extra-curricular activities, and they froze to death. How many times has Russia been saved by the weather?

The New York Times *interview, July 19, 2017, talking about his visit with France's president Emmanuel Macron*

> War is life multiplied by some number that no one has ever heard of.
>
> Sebastian Junger, *War*

Wherever this vessel cuts through the horizon our allies will rest easy and our enemies will shake with fear because everyone will know that America is coming and America is coming strong.

Speaking at the commissioning ceremony for the USS Gerald R. Ford *in Norfolk, Virginia. This was a prepared speech.*

> In less than an hour I have to hold class for a group of idiot freshmen. And, on a desk in the living room, is a mountain of midterm examinations with essays I must suffer through, feeling my stomach turn at their paucity of intelligence, their adolescent phraseology.
>
> Richard Matheson, *Collected Stories*, Vol. 1

The people who were questioning that statement, "was it too tough," maybe it wasn't tough enough. They have been doing this to our country for a long time, for many years. It us about time someone stuck up for the people of other country (*sic*). If anything, maybe that statement wasn't tough enough and we are backed by 100 percent by our military, we are backed by everybody and we are backed by many other leaders.

Trump's follow-up statement about the bellicose remarks he made the previous day about North Korea: "They will be met with fire and fury like the world has never seen." August 8, 2017.

> If you want to release your aggression, get up and dance. That's what rock and roll is all about.
>
> Chuck Berry

Many great American soldiers, both of the North and South, died at this spot, "the Rapids," on the Potomac River. The casualties were so great that the water would turn red and thus became known as "The River of Blood." It is my great honor to have preserved this important section of the Potomac River!

Plaque signed by Donald J. Trump at his Virginia golf course, commemorating a Civil War battle that never happened.

> One of the saddest lessons of history is this: If we've been bamboozled long enough, we tend to reject any evidence of the bamboozle. We're no longer interested in finding out the truth. The bamboozle has captured us. It's simply too painful

to acknowledge, even to ourselves, that we've been taken. Once you give a charlatan power over you, you almost never get it back.

Carl Sagan, *The Demon-Haunted World: Science as a Candle in the Dark*

The Environment and Science

In all the ways that matter, Trump holds and promotes anti-scientific views. He doubts humans cause global warming, and he demonstrated that belief by appointing Scott Pruitt, a man who doesn't believe carbon dioxide or human activity cause global warming, as head of the Environmental Protection Agency. Pruitt said, "I think that measuring with precision human activity on the climate is something very challenging to do and there's tremendous disagreement about the degree of impact. So no, I would not agree that it's a primary contributor to the global warming that we see."

Rick Perry occupies the Energy Department's Secretary seat. He also denies the primary role of carbon dioxide in global warming. Perry said, "Most likely the primary control knob is the ocean waters and this environment that we live in."

As of the writing of this book, Trump still hasn't appointed a science advisor.

Trump's proposed 2018 budget[2] slashes science as if science were optional for progress. He wants to cut:

- 18 percent of the National Institute of Health's budget
- 13 percent of the U.S. Geological Survey's budget
- 8.7 percent of NASA's earth science budget
- 31 percent of the Food and Drug Administration budget
- 11 percent of the National Science Foundation's budget

And more, but you get the idea.

What does this mean in human terms? Take earthquakes, for example. Trump's proposed budget eliminates funds for an earthquake early warning system for California. Japan and Mexico have advanced early warning systems that save lives. When it comes to earthquakes, even a few seconds' warning can save lives. A few seconds is enough time for surgeons to remove instruments from inside a patient, for elevators to stop, and for the general public to take cover.

Trump's budget calls for an eighty-two percent cut to Regional Climate Centers that provide essential forecasting and resources for everything from helping

---

2. See http://www.sciencemag.org/news/2017/05/what-s-trump-s-2018-budget-request-science and https://www.theverge.com/2017/5/23/15682188/trump-science-budget-nih-cdc-nsf-epa-doe-energy-research-funding-cuts for more on Trump's science budget cuts.

farmers determine when to plant crops to fighting wildfires. Proposed budget cuts to the National Oceanic and Atmospheric Administration will put fewer weather satellites in orbit, and the proposed cuts to the National Weather Service will slow the development of advanced weather forecasting tools. In short, Trump wants weather forecasting to become less accurate and timely, a brazen step backwards.

Science is about progress and saving lives. But not under Donald Trump.

With the coldest winter ever recorded, with snow setting record levels up and down the coast, the Nobel committee should take the Nobel Prize back from Al Gore. . . . Gore wants us to clean up our factories and plants in order to protect us from global warming, when China and other countries couldn't care less. It would make us totally noncompetitive in the manufacturing world, and China, Japan and India are laughing at America's stupidity.

Trump speaking at one of his golf clubs in 2010. Trump, like other climate change deniers, equates short-term, seasonal weather with climate. The two are unrelated. But never mind that: China, Japan, and India signed the Paris climate accord. The United States did, too, until President Trump announced he would withdraw America as soon as he is legally able to do so, in 2019. .

> The Norwegian Nobel Committee rarely raises its voice. Our style is largely sober. But it is a long time since the committee was concerned with such fundamental questions as this year. Desmond Tutu, Peace Prize Laureate in 1984, put it as follows in Tromsø's Arctic Cathedral in connection with World Environment Day on the 5th of June: "To ignore the challenge of global warming may be criminal. It certainly is disobeying God. It is sin. The future of our fragile, beautiful planet is in our hands. We are stewards of God's creation."
>
> We congratulate the IPCC [Intergovernmental Panel on Climate Change] and Al Gore on receiving this year's Peace Prize. We thank you for what

> you have done for mother earth, and wish you further success in a task that is so vital to us all.
>
> *Nobel Prize Committee, 2007*

The concept of global warming was created by and for the Chinese.

Tweet, November 7, 2002

> If you look at the history of climate change negotiations, actually it was initiated by the IPCC [Intergovernmental Panel on Climate Change] with the support of the Republicans during the Reagan and senior Bush administration during the late 1980s.
>
> China's Vice Foreign Minister Liu Zhenmin, November, 17, 2016

I believe in clean air. Immaculate air. . . . But I don't believe in climate change.

CNN interview, September 24, 2015

> The whole problem with the world is that fools and fanatics are always so certain of themselves, and wiser people so full of doubts.
>
> Bertrand Russell

Ice storm rolls from Texas to Tennessee—I'm in Los Angeles and it's freezing. Global warming is a total, and very expensive, hoax!

Tweet, December 7, 2013

> We have many advantages in the fight against global warming, but time is not one of them. Instead of idly debating the precise extent of global warming, or the precise timeline of global warming, we need to deal with the central facts of rising temperatures, rising waters, and all the endless troubles that global warming will bring. We stand warned by serious and credible scientists across the world that time is short and the dangers are great. The most relevant question now is whether our own government is equal to the challenge.
>
> Senator John McCain, September 12, 2008

I am totally in favor of vaccines. But I want smaller doses over a longer period of time. Same exact amount, but you take this little beautiful baby, and you pump—mean, it looks just like it's meant for a horse, not for a child, and we've had so many instances, people that work for me, ... [in which] a child, a beautiful child went to have the vaccine, and came back and a week later had a tremendous fever, got very, very sick, now is autistic.

During the Republican Party primary presidential debate, September 2015. Andrew Wakefield was the British physician whose completely discredited study set off the wave of paranoia about vaccines. Wakefield, who was stripped of his license to practice medicine, made an appearance at one of Donald Trump's inaugural balls.

> Vaccines save lives; fear endangers them. It's a simple message parents need to keep hearing.
>
> Jeffrey Kluger, *Time Magazine*, November 4, 2010

This very expensive GLOBAL WARMING bullshit has got to stop. Our planet is freezing, record low temps, and our GW scientists are stuck in ice

Tweet, January 2, 2014

> When you have people who don't know much about science standing in denial of it and rising to power, that is a recipe for the complete dismantling of our informed democracy.
>
> Neil deGrasse Tyson

Obama's talking about all of this with the global warming and . . . a lot of it's a hoax. It's a hoax. I mean, it's a money-making industry, okay? It's a hoax, a lot of it.

Campaign rally, December 2015

> So the carnival steams by, shakes ANY tree: it rains jackasses.
>
> Ray Bradbury, *Something Wicked This Way Comes*

I think right now. . . . well, I think there is some connectivity. There is some, something. It depends on how much. It also depends on how much it's going to cost our companies. You have to understand, our companies are noncompetitive right now.

New York Times *interview, November 23, 2016, in response to James Bennett's question, "When you say an open mind, you mean you're just not sure whether human activity causes climate change? Do you think human activity is or isn't connected?"*

> The future is there. . . . looking back at us. Trying to make sense of the fiction we will have become.
>
> William Gibson, *Pattern Recognition*

Guns, Safety and Violence

I was struck by a number I read in an article: one. That's the number of people murdered by gun in Japan in 2015. In the same year, 13,286 Americans were murdered by firearms. Wrap your head around that staggering difference for a moment.

Living in Japan isn't risk-free, of course. In the March 2011 earthquake, 15,891 people died. Earthquakes are a terrifying danger here, and there's a big one on the way in which hundreds of thousands of people could perish. Nobody wants to die in an earthquake, but fortunately we can take steps to keep ourselves alive. New buildings are earthquake-resistant, elevators have emergency supplies, offices stock food and water for their employees, earthquake alarms give valuable seconds of warning, everyone knows his or her nearest evacuation center, and people have several days' worth of food, water, and other supplies in their homes.

But when it comes to guns, short of wearing a bulletproof vest, there's nothing you can do to keep yourself from becoming a random death statistic.

The main difference between gun and earthquake safety is this: In Japan, people and the government have the will, imagination, and motivation to prevent unnecessary death. When it comes to guns, America still shrugs its shoulders.

Donald Trump is a steadfast supporter of gun rights. His views are unwavering, unimaginative, and ultimately predictable. We'll get no change, no progress with gun safety during Donald Trump's reign.

The right of self-defense doesn't stop at the end of your driveway. . . . A driver's license works in every state, so it's common sense that a concealed carry permit should work in every state.

Breitbart News, September 18, 2015

> Speaking personally, you can have my gun, but you'll take my book when you pry my cold, dead fingers off of the binding.
>
> Stephen King

I could stand in the middle of Fifth Avenue and shoot somebody and I wouldn't lose any voters.

During a campaign speech in Iowa, January 24, 2016. During the campaign and continuing into his presidency, Trump made calls and innuendos to violence. On July 2, 2017, for instance, Trump posted a tweet with a GIF showing him punching a man with the CNN logo on his face.

> Violence is the last refuge of the incompetent.
>
> Isaac Asimov, *Foundation*

You know what I hate? There's a guy, totally disruptive, throwing punches. We're not allowed to punch back anymore. I love the old days. You know what they used to do to guys like that when they were in a place like this? They'd be carried out on a stretcher, folks. Ah, it's true . . . I'd like to punch him in the face, I'll tell you.

At a campaign rally in Las Vegas, February 22, 2016

> I am a violent man who has learned not to be violent and regrets his violence.
>
> John Lennon

We have a situation where we have our inner cities, African-Americans, Hispanics are living in hell because it's so dangerous. You walk down the street, you get shot.

Presidential debate, September 2016

> The Constitution gives you the right, as a white man, to have a rifle in your home. The Constitution gives you the right to protect yourself. Why is it "ominous" when black people even talk of having rifles? Why don't we have the right to self-defense? Is it because maybe you know we're going to have to defend ourselves against you?
>
> James Baldwin, *One Day When I Was Lost*

I have the endorsement of the NRA which I'm very proud of, these are very, very good people and they're protecting the Second Amendment.

Presidential debate, September 2016. In 2014, there were 33,599 gun deaths in the United States. In the same year, in Japan, there were six.

> Almost no one in Japan owns a gun. Most kinds are illegal, with onerous restrictions on buying and maintaining the few that are allowed. Even the country's infamous, mafia-like Yakuza tend to forgo guns; the few exceptions tend to become big national news stories.
>
> To get a gun in Japan, first, you have to attend an all-day class and pass a written test, which are held only once per month. You also must take and pass a shooting range class. Then, head over to a hospital for a mental test and drug test (Japan is unusual in that potential gun owners must affirmatively prove their mental fitness), which you'll file with the police. Finally, pass a rigorous background check for any criminal record or association with criminal or extremist groups, and you will be the proud new owner of your shotgun or air rifle. Just don't forget to provide police with documentation on the specific location of the gun in your home, as well as the ammo, both of which must be locked and stored separately. And remember to have the police inspect the gun once per year and to re-take the class and exam every three years.
>
> Max Fisher, *The Atlantic*, July 23, 2012

I'm very much in favor of making all concealed-carry permits valid in every state. Every state has its own driving test that residents have to pass before becoming licensed to drive. Those tests are different in many states, but once a state licenses you to drive, every other state recognizes that license as valid.

If we can do that for driving—which is a privilege, not a right—then surely we can do that for concealed carry, which is a right, not a privilege. That seems logical to me.

Crippled America, *2015*

> Every day in America is a day with a shooting.
>
> Bill Maher

When you look at Paris—you know the toughest gun laws in the world, Paris—nobody had guns but the bad guys. Nobody had guns. Nobody. They were just shooting them one by one and then they [security forces] broke in and had a big shootout and ultimately killed the terrorists. You can say what you want, but if they had guns, if our people had guns, if they were allowed to carry—it would've been a much, much different situation.

After the Bataclan attack in Paris, 2015

> Common-sense is part of the home-made ideology of those who have been deprived of fundamental learning, of those who have been kept ignorant.

> This ideology is compounded from different sources: items that have survived from religion, items of empirical knowledge, items of protective skepticism, items culled for comfort from the superficial learning that is supplied. But the point is that common-sense can never teach itself, can never advance beyond its own limits, for as soon as the lack of fundamental learning has been made good, all items become questionable and the whole function of common-sense is destroyed. Common-sense can only exist as a category insofar as it can be distinguished from the spirit of inquiry, from philosophy.
>
> John Berger

The gun-free zones are target practice for the sickos and for the mentally ill. They look for gun-free zones. The six soldiers that were killed. Two of them were among the most highly decorated, and they weren't allowed on a military base to have guns. And somebody walked in and shot them, killed them. If they had guns, he wouldn't be around very long. I can tell you, there wouldn't have been much damage. I think gun-free zones are a catastrophe. They're a feeding frenzy for sick people.

Republican debate, Oct 28, 2015

> We lose eight children and teenagers to gun violence every day. If a mysterious virus suddenly

started killing eight of our children every day, America would mobilize teams of doctors and public health officials. We would move heaven and earth until we found a way to protect our children. But not with gun violence.

Elizabeth Warren, *A Fighting Chance*

Do you notice we are not having a gun debate right now? That's because they used knives and a truck!

Tweet June 4, 2017, in response to a terrorist attack in London that used knives and a truck. Eight people were killed, 28 injured. More would have likely died if the terrorists had guns.

We must become bigger than we have been: more courageous, greater in spirit, larger in outlook. We must become members of a new race, overcoming petty prejudice, owing our ultimate allegiance not to nations but to our fellow men within the human community.

Haile Selassie, Ethiopia's emperor from 1930 to 1974

Money, Wealth and Those Who Don't Have Much

"Greed is right, greed works. Greed clarifies, cuts through, and captures the essence of the evolutionary spirit. Greed, in all of its forms; greed for life, for money, for love, knowledge has marked the upward surge of mankind. And greed, you mark my words, will not only save Teldar Paper, but that other malfunctioning corporation called the USA."

Gordon Gekko (played by Michael Douglas) from the 1987 movie Wall Street.

Image a billionaire president. Now imagine that president brings his family members, who work with him in business and who are multimillionaires in their own right, into the White House. Imagine further that this president doesn't sever his ties to his business as he carries out his oath and duties as President of the United States. And one more item for your imagination: This president owns properties for which the government pays him rent.

Trump steers the ship of state into uncharted, unethical, and likely unconstitutional waters—all so he can continue to enrich himself. The framers were wise to bar officials from accepting gifts or money from foreign countries. The United States Constitution says, "No Person holding any Office of Profit or Trust under them, shall, without the Consent of the Congress, accept of any present, Emolument, Office, or Title, of any kind whatever, from any King, Prince, or foreign State." There is debate as to whether Donald Trump accepting income in the form of hotel room rentals from foreign governments is unconstitutional (in part because the Emoluments Clause has never been tested this way before). But what is clear is that foreign governments are consciously renting rooms in Trump hotels, including Washington, DC's Trump International Hotel, to curry favor with the president. What's also clear is that Trump could have separated himself from his businesses when he became president, removing all ethical and financial entanglements.

Trump chose not to put his businesses and holdings into a blind trust as other presidents have done. Why? Because greed flows through Trump the way that blood flows through ordinary people's veins. Trump is using the presidency to siphon as much money as he can from the pockets of American taxpayers and into his own. As Trump himself said, "You can never be too greedy."

The point is, you can never be too greedy.

In The Art of the Deal. *Of all of Trump's philosophies, he's kept most true to this one.*

> There is more in you of good than you know, child of the kindly West. Some courage and some wisdom, blended in measure. If more of us valued food and cheer and song above hoarded gold, it would be a merrier world.
>
> J.R.R. Tolkien, *The Hobbit*

My entire life, I've watched politicians bragging about how poor they are, how they came from nothing, how poor their parents and grandparents were. And I said to myself, if they can stay so poor for so many generations, maybe this isn't the kind of person we want to be electing to higher office. How smart can they be? They're morons.

1999 interview with Maureen Dowd in The New York Times

> There is always more misery among the lower classes than there is humanity in the higher.
>
> Victor Hugo, *Les Misérables*

Part of the beauty of me is that I am very rich.

Good Morning America, 2011

> Whoever loves money never has enough; whoever loves wealth is never satisfied with their income. This too is meaningless.
>
> Ecclesiastes 5:10

I would save the middle class. I know what to do. Our jobs are all being taken out of our country.

Breitbart News Sunday, *May 2015*

> How can you be somebody else's savior, when you can't be your own?
>
> Caroline B. Cooney

Somebody said, "Why did you appoint a rich person to be in charge of the economy?" No, it's true. And [Commerce Secretary Ross,] a very rich person in charge of commerce. I said: "Because that's the kind of thinking we want." . . . And I love all people, rich or poor, but in those particular positions I just don't want a poor person. Does that make sense?

Cedar Rapids, Iowa, June 2017. Actually, it doesn't make sense that only rich people should set economic policy.

> If you're in trouble, or hurt or need, go to the poor people. They're the only ones that'll help, the only ones.
>
> John Steinbeck, *The Grapes of Wrath*

I've done it four times out of hundreds, and I'm glad I did it. I used the laws of the country to my benefit.

Republican debate, October 28, 2015, talking about how used bankruptcy laws to his advantage.

> The few own the many because they possess the means of livelihood of all. . . . The country is governed for the richest, for the corporations, the bankers, the land speculators, and for the exploiters of labor. The majority of mankind are working people. So long as their fair demands—the ownership and control of their livelihoods—are set at naught, we can have neither men's rights nor women's rights. The majority of mankind is

> ground down by industrial oppression in order that the small remnant may live in ease.
>
> Helen Keller, *Rebel Lives: Helen Keller*

I understand debt better than probably anybody. I know how to deal with debt very well. I love debt—but you know, debt is tricky and it's dangerous, and you have to be careful and you have to know what you're doing.

CNN interview, May 10, 2016

> He was out to get back everything he'd lost; there was no end to his loss; this thing would drag on forever.
>
> Jack Kerouac, *On the Road*

I don't know. That's a very interesting question. I doubt it. I doubt it. Because they're not going to . . . nobody cares about my tax return except for the reporters. Oh, at some point I'll release them. Maybe I'll release them after I'm finished because I'm very proud of them actually. I did a good job . . .

By the way, so as you know I'm under routine audit, so they're not going to be done. But you know, at a certain point, that's something I will consider. But I would never consider it as part of a deal . . .

I would never do it. That would be . . . I think that would be unfair to the deal. It would be disrespectful of the importance of this deal. Because the only people that find that important are the reporters.

Response to a question if Trump would release his tax returns as condition for getting his tax plan through Congress, The Economist interview, May 11, 2017. Trump said, "I'm very proud of them," words that likely no one has ever said about tax returns.

> The man who lies to himself and listens to his own lie comes to such a pass that he cannot distinguish the truth within him.
>
> Fyodor Dostoevsky, *The Brothers Karamazov*

But I built up a net worth of much more than $10 billion, net worth, that means net worth.

The Economist *interview, September 3, 2017*

> It is well enough that people of the nation do not understand our banking and monetary system, for if they did, I believe there would be a revolution before tomorrow morning.
>
> Henry Ford

For all those who want to #MakeAmericaGreatAgain, boycott @Macys. They are weak on border security & stopping illegal immigration.

Tweet, July 1, 2015, reacting angrily to Macy's decision to stop carrying Trump's ties and men's cologne, which Macy's did after Trump's remarks calling Mexican immigrants rapists and drug dealers.

> We learn our lessons; we get hurt; we want revenge. Then we realize that actually, happiness and forgiving people is the best revenge.
>
> Madonna

It has not been easy for me. It has not been easy for me. And, you know, I started off in Brooklyn. My father gave me a small loan of a million dollars.

Today *interview with Matt Lauer, NBC, October 26, 2015*

> It is not the creation of wealth that is wrong, but the love of money for its own sake.
>
> Margaret Thatcher

I settled the Trump University lawsuit for a small fraction of the potential award because as President I have to focus on our country.

The ONLY bad thing about winning the Presidency is that I did not have the time to go through a long but winning trial on Trump U. Too bad!

Two tweets on November 19, 2016

> All other swindlers upon earth are nothing to the self-swindlers, and with such pretences did I cheat myself. Surely a curious thing. That I should innocently take a bad half-crown of somebody else's manufacture, is reasonable enough; but that I should knowingly reckon the spurious coin of my own make, as good money!
>
> Charles Dickens, *Great Expectations*

He loaned me a small amount of money—loaned, not gave—around $1 million—money that I probably could have gotten from a bank—and the biggest part of my journey began. I paid my father back a few years later, with full interest, after my Manhattan deals started to come in—and very successfully.

Crippled America, *on the loan he received from his father*

Dr. Evil: Shit. Oh hell, let's just do what we always do. Hijack some nuclear weapons and hold the world hostage. Yeah? Good! Gentlemen, it has come to my attention that a breakaway Russian Republic called Kreplachistan will be transferring a nuclear warhead to the United Nations in a few days. Here's the plan. We get the warhead and we hold the world ransom for one million dollars!

Number Two: Don't you think we should ask for more than a million dollars? A million dollars isn't exactly a lot of money these days. Virtucon alone makes over 9 billion dollars a year!

Dr. Evil: Really? That's a lot of money.

Dr. Evil: Okay then, we hold the world ransom for one hundred billion dollars!

Dr. Evil in *Austin Powers: International Man of Mystery* (1997)

Not-White, and Not-Trump

If you're not like Trump—that is, white and male—chances are he's insulted you, diminished you, or doesn't think about you. Trump's harsh words about Hispanics became his most famous of the campaign. His strange use of phrases like "the blacks," and "my African-Americans" are cringeworthy.

In February 2016, during a CNN interview with Jake Tapper, Trump tried to deny knowing anything about David Duke, former Grand Dragon of the Ku Klux Klan and an active white nationalist:

> *Well, just so you understand, I don't know anything about David Duke. Okay? I don't know anything about what you're even talking about with white supremacy or white supremacists. So, I don't know . . .*

> *I don't know, did he endorse me or what's going on, because, you know, I know nothing about David Duke. I know nothing about white supremacists. And so you're asking me a question that I'm supposed to be talking about people that I know nothing about. . . .*
>
> *I don't know any—honestly, I don't know David Duke. I don't believe I have ever met him. I'm pretty sure I didn't meet him. And I just don't know anything about him.*

Honestly? Honestly, who in America doesn't know about David Duke, especially if you're in politics? In 1991 and 2000, Trump specifically talked about David Duke (and at the time made statements opposing Duke). "I don't know anything about David Duke" is a as pure a lie as any Trump has told.

When asked in a later interview with NBC's John Heilemann, Trump, when prodded, disavowed the endorsement, but did so in a mealy, crafty way:

> *Sure, I would do that if it made you feel better. I would certainly repudiate. I don't know anything about him. Somebody told me yesterday, whoever he is, he did endorse me. And actually I don't think it was an endorsement. He said I was absolutely the best of all the candidates. But I wouldn't want him.*

Notice the word, "would." Trump didn't say "I repudiate;" instead he used a conditional. He said he would repudiate "if it made you feel better." Trump pointed out: "He said I was absolutely the best of all the candidates," which is not something you say when you're disavowing a racist. This disavowal wasn't a repudiation at all. It was a wink to white nationalists that said, "I'm in your corner, no matter what the press tries to get me to say."

It matters, too, that David Duke, America's leading white nationalist, endorses Trump because he thinks that Trump's policies and those of white nationalists are in alignment. Duke called Trump's 2016 election victory "one of the most exciting nights of [his] life."

On August 12, 2017, white supremacists marched in Charlottesville, Virginia to protest the removal of a statue of Confederate General Robert E. Lee. (Calling these people mere white supremacists is a watering down of what they are: neo-Nazis. People who chant Nazi-era slogans and give Nazi salutes are Nazis.) The demonstration turned violent and one woman was killed. Trump offered this milquetoast response: "We condemn in the strongest possible terms this egregious display of hatred, bigotry and violence on many sides—on many sides. It's been going on for a long time in our country. Not Donald Trump, not Barack Obama. It's been going on for a long, long time. It has no place in America." Notice that Trump said, "on many sides," which was not only not true, but was an unsubtle wink to his base of bigots and racists. In two tweets, Trump added, "We must remember this truth: No matter our color, creed, religion or political party, we are ALL AMERICANS FIRST. Condolences to the family of the young woman killed today, and best regards to all of those injured, in Charlottesville, Virginia. So sad!"

America's racists noticed the wink. (So did everyone else.) "Trump's comments were good. He didn't attack us. He just said the nation should come together. Nothing specific against us. . . . No condemnation at all. When asked to condemn, he just walked out of the room. Really,

really good. God bless him," wrote *The Daily Stormer*, a white supremacist website.

Days later, Trump held a press conference in which he doubled down on his remarks, going off the rails, in the views of many, including me. Among other things, Trump equated Robert E. Lee and Stonewall Jackson with George Washington and Thomas Jefferson, saying on August 16, 2017, "[M]any of those people were there to protest the taking down of the statue of Robert E. Lee. So this week, it is Robert E. Lee. I noticed that Stonewall Jackson is coming down. I wonder, is it George Washington next week? And is it Thomas Jefferson the week after? You know, you really do have to ask yourself, where does it stop?" Where to begin with this one? I'll just say that one big difference between these Confederate generals and Washington and Jefferson is that they waged war on the United States, while Washington and Jefferson were involved in its founding.

The racism and xenophobia in Trump's now infamous December 2015 clarion call, "Donald J. Trump is calling for a total and complete shutdown of Muslims entering the United States until our country's representatives can figure out what is going on," will forever be a stain on America. Trump speaks to exclusion in the exact opposite way the Statue of Liberty calls for inclusion: "Give me your tired, your poor,/ Your huddled masses yearning to breathe free/, The wretched refuse of your teeming shore,/ Send these, the homeless, tempest-tost to me,/ I lift my lamp beside the golden door!"

Trump has surrounded himself with a bubble of people with a history of bigotry. In 1986, the Senate refused to confirm Trump's now-Attorney General, Jeffrey Sessions, as a federal judge because Sessions said the only reason he hadn't joined the Ku Klux Klan was because KKK members smoked marijuana. Steve Bannon, Trump's campaign strategist and confidant, was the former executive chairman of Breitbart News, a publication supportive of many white nationalist goals. Under Bannon's leadership, Breitbart published articles with titles like, "Would You Rather Your Child Had Feminism or Cancer?"

You can tell a lot about somebody by what they say. You can tell a lot about somebody by the company they keep. And you can tell a whole lot about somebody by both of these.

Jeb Bush has to like the Mexican Illegals because of his wife.

Tweet, July 4, 2015. This tweet was retweeted by Trump and then deleted.

> Are Latino-Americans white? Black? Other? Illegal aliens from Mars? Or are we the very face of America?
>
> Raquel Cepeda, *Bird of Paradise: How I Became Latina*

We condemn in the strongest possible terms this egregious display of hatred, bigotry and violence on many sides—on many sides. It's been going on for a long time in our country. Not Donald Trump, not Barack Obama. It's been going on for a long, long time. It has no place in America.

August 12, in response to white supremacist violence in Charlottesville, Virginia in which one person was killed. "On many sides" will go down in history as code for bigotry and racism.

> It was not, however, to these Fascist groups, numerically unimportant as they were, that the Third Republic owed its collapse. On the contrary, the plain, if paradoxical, truth is that their influence was never so slight as at the moment

> when the collapse actually took place. What made France fall was the fact that she had no more true Dreyfusards, no one who believed that democracy and freedom, equality and justice could any longer be defended or realized under the republic.
>
> Hannah Arendt, *The Origins of Totalitarianism*, 1951

Look at my African American over here! Are you the greatest? Do you know what I'm talking about?

Campaign rally, June 3, 2016

> Yeah, I love being famous. It's almost like being white, y'know?
>
> Chris Rock

I've been treated very unfairly by this judge. Now, this judge is of Mexican heritage. I'm building a wall, okay? I'm building a wall. I am going to do very well with the Hispanics, the Mexicans. . . .

I think I'm going to do very well with Hispanics. But we're building a wall. He's a Mexican. We're building a wall between here and Mexico. This judge is giving us unfair rulings. Now I say why. Well, I want to—I'm building a wall, okay? And it's a wall between Mexico, not another country.

CNN interview in which Trump condemned U.S. District Judge Gonzalo Curiel, who was presiding over the fraud trial about Trump University, June 3, 2016. Judge Curiel was born in Indiana.

> It would be interesting to find out what goes on in that moment when someone looks at you and draws all sorts of conclusions.
>
> Malcolm Gladwell

I have a great relationship with the blacks. I've always had a great relationship with the blacks.

April 2011 radio interview with Talk1300, Albany, NY

> "Scout," said Atticus, "nigger-lover is just one of those terms that don't mean anything—like snot-nose. It's hard to explain—ignorant, trashy people use it when they think somebody's favoring Negroes over and above themselves. It's slipped into usage with some people like ourselves, when they want a common, ugly term to label somebody."
>
> "You aren't really a nigger-lover, then, are you?"
>
> "I certainly am. I do my best to love everybody . . . I'm hard put, sometimes—baby, it's never

> an insult to be called what somebody thinks is a bad name. It just shows you how poor that person is, it doesn't hurt you."
>
> Harper Lee, *To Kill a Mockingbird*

When these people walk in the room, they don't say, "Oh, hello! How's the weather? It's so beautiful outside. Isn't it lovely? How are the Yankees doing? Oh they're doing wonderful. Great." They say, "We want deal!"

Talking about Asians at a rally in Iowa, August 2015

> I met a woman who told me that she wasn't attracted to Asians. "No worries," I said. "I'm not attracted to racists."
>
> Simon S. Tam

A well-educated black has a tremendous advantage over a well-educated white in terms of the job market. . . . If I was starting off today, I would love to be a well-educated black, because I really do believe they have the actual advantage today.

Interview with Bryant Gumbel in 1989

> The straitjackets of race prejudice and discrimination do not wear only southern labels. The subtle, psychological technique of the North has approached in its ugliness and victimization of the Negro the outright terror and open brutality of the South.
>
> Martin Luther King, Jr., *Why We Can't Wait*

[M]any of those people were there to protest the taking down of the statue of Robert E. Lee. So this week, it is Robert E. Lee. I noticed that Stonewall Jackson is coming down. I wonder, is it George Washington next week? And is it Thomas Jefferson the week after? You know, you really do have to ask yourself, where does it stop?

Press conference, August 16, 2017

> I absolutely refuse to associate myself with anyone who cannot discern the essential night-and-day difference between theocratic fascism and liberal secular democracy, even less do I want to engage with those who are incapable of recognizing the basic moral distinction between premeditated mass murder and unintentional killing.
>
> Christopher Hitchens, *Christopher Hitchens and His Critics: Terror, Iraq, and the Left*

That's right, we need a TRAVEL BAN for certain DANGEROUS countries, not some politically correct term that won't help us protect our people!

Tweet, June 6 2017

> You can safely assume you've created God in your own image when it turns out that God hates all the same people you do.
>
> Anne Lamott

IN AMERICA WE DON'T WORSHIP GOVERNMENT—WE WORSHIP GOD!

Tweet, July 26, 2017

> Congress shall make no law respecting an establishment of religion, or prohibiting the free exercise thereof.
>
> United States Constitution

I don't see how there is any room for misunderstanding or misinterpretation of the statement I made on June 16th during my Presidential announcement speech. What can be simpler or more accurately stated? The Mexican government is forcing their most unwanted people into the United States. They are, in many cases, criminals, drug dealers, rapists, etc.

July 6, 2015

> When the reader can't know what's being omitted and it's not clear that there are more items in the list, etc. may signal laziness or dishonesty. In lazy moments, some writers use etc. when they know of only one or two examples but want to create the impression that there are more. Any engaged reader can see through this trick.
>
> Grammarist

The largest suppliers of heroin, cocaine and other illicit drugs are Mexican cartels that arrange to have Mexican immigrants trying to cross the borders and smuggle in the drugs. The Border Patrol knows this. Likewise, tremendous infectious disease is pouring across the border.

Statement released on July 6, 2015

> There is another class of coloured people who make a business of keeping the troubles, the wrongs, and the hardships of the Negro race before the public. Having learned that they are able to make a living out of their troubles, they have grown into the

> settled habit of advertising their wrongs—partly because they want sympathy and partly because it pays. Some of these people do not want the Negro to lose his grievances, because they do not want to lose their jobs.
>
> Booker T. Washington

Even the president of Mexico called me. Their southern border, they said very few people are coming because they know they're not going to get to our border, which is the ultimate compliment.

Claiming that he was praised by President Enrique Peña Nieto of Mexico for his strong words against illegal immigration in a speech to the Boy Scouts, August 31, 2017. The Mexican president's office issued this statement in response: "President Enrique Peña Nieto has not had any recent telephone communication with President Donald Trump."

> In one aspect, yes, I believe in ghosts, but we create them. We haunt ourselves.
>
> Laurie Halse Anderson, *Wintergirls*

Thank you to the LGBT community! I will fight for you while Hillary brings in more people that will threaten your freedoms and beliefs.

Tweet, June 15, 2016. On July 26, 2917, Trump, seemingly out of the blue, tweeted that transgender Americans would no longer be allowed to serve in the military.

> They don't choose to be transgender. . . . Why should we hold that against them?
>
> Senator Orrin Hatch, on MSNBC, July 27, 2017, responding to Donald Trump's decision to ban transgender Americans from serving in the military.

Well, just so you understand, I don't know anything about David Duke, okay? I don't know anything about what you're even talking about with white supremacy or white supremacists. So, I don't know. I don't know, did he endorse me, or what's going on? Because, you know, I know nothing about David Duke. I know nothing about white supremacists. And so you're asking me a question that I'm supposed to be talking about people that I know nothing about.

Interview on CNN with Jake Tapper, February 28, 2016, responding to a question about whether he would disavow David Duke and other white supremacist groups that were supporting Trump's candidacy. On February 14, 2000, Trump called David Duke "a big racist." So much for not knowing anything about Duke.

> Well, you've got David Duke just joined—a bigot, a racist, a problem. I mean, this is not exactly the people you want in your party.
>
> Trump on NBC's the *Today Show*, February 14, 2000

It is a great honor to be here with all of my friends—so amazing & will never forget!

Trump's inscription in the Yad Vashem visitor's book, May 2017. Yad Vashem is the memorial to the Holocaust in Israel.

> I am grateful to Yad Vashem and all of those responsible for this remarkable institution. At a time of great peril and promise, war and strife, we are blessed to have such a powerful reminder of man's potential for great evil, but also our capacity to rise up from tragedy and remake our world. Let our children come here, and know this history, so that they can add their voices to proclaim "never again".
>
> And may we remember those who perished, not only as victims, but also as individuals who hoped and loved and dreamed like us, and who have become symbols of the human spirit.
>
> Barack Obama's inscription in Yad Vashem's visitor book, 2008

I wonder if President Obama would have attended the funeral of Justice Scalia if it were held in a Mosque? Very sad that he did not go!

Twitter, February 21, 2016

> "What is it you most dislike?" Stupidity, especially in its nastiest forms of racism and superstition.
>
> Christopher Hitchens, *Hitch-22: A Memoir*

I'm a negotiator—like you folks . . . Is there anybody that doesn't renegotiate deals in this room? Perhaps more than any room I've ever spoken to.

Speaking to Jewish Republican donors in 2015

> Can anything be more disgusting than to hear people called 'educated' making small jokes about eating ham, and showing themselves empty of any real knowledge as to the relation of their own social and religious life to the history of the people they think themselves witty in insulting? . . . The best thing that can be said of it is, that it is a sign of the intellectual narrowness—in plain English, the stupidity which is still the average mark of our culture.
>
> George Eliot

People, the lawyers and the courts can call it whatever they want, but I am calling it what we need and what it is, a TRAVEL BAN!

Tweet, June 5, 2017

> The fact that the Hegnish have absolutely no interest in any people except themselves can also cause offense, or even rage. Foreigners exist. That is all the Hegnish know about them, and all they care to know. They are too polite to say that it is a pity that foreigners exist, but if they had to think about it, they would think so.
>
> Ursula K. Le Guin, *Changing Planes*

The illegal immigrants . . . have taken jobs that should go to people here legally, while over 20 percent of Americans are currently unemployed.

Crippled America

> The land flourished because it was fed from so many sources because it was nourished by so many cultures and traditions and peoples.
>
> Lyndon B. Johnson

Believe me, if I run and I win, I will be the greatest representative of the Christians they've had in a long time.

Christian Broadcasting Network interview with David Brody, May 20, 2015

> Almost any sect, cult, or religion will legislate its creed into law if it acquires the political power to do so.
>
> Robert A. Heinlein

As far as the lawsuit, yes, when I was very young, I went into my father's real estate company in Brooklyn and Queens, and we, along with many, many other companies throughout the country—it was a federal lawsuit—were sued. We settled the suit with no admission of guilt. I'll go one step further. In Palm Beach, Florida, a wealthy community, I opened a club, and really got great credit for it: no discrimination against African-Americans, against Muslims, against anybody.

Presidential debate, Sep 26, 2016. In 1973 the Justice Department initiated a civil rights lawsuit against Trump's rental management company, which he and his father owned, for refusing to rent to African-Americans and Puerto Ricans.

> I feel that for white America to understand the significance of the problem of the Negro will take

a bigger and tougher America than any we have yet known. I feel that America's past is too shallow, her national character too superficially optimistic, her very morality too suffused with color hate for her to accomplish so vast and complex a task.

Culturally the Negro represents a paradox: Though he is an organic part of the nation, he is excluded by the ride and direction of American culture. Frankly, it is felt to be right to exclude him, and it is felt to be wrong to admit him freely. Therefore if, within the confines of its present culture, the nation ever seeks to purge itself of its color hate, it will find itself at war with itself, convulsed by a spasm of emotional and moral confusion.

If the nation ever finds itself examining its real relation to the Negro, it will find itself doing infinitely more than that; for the anti-Negro attitude of whites represents but a tiny part—though a symbolically significant one—of the moral attitude of the nation. Our too-young and too-new America, lusty because it is lonely, aggressive because it is afraid, insists upon seeing the world in terms of good and bad, the holy and the evil, the high and the low, the white and the black; our America is frightened of fact, of history, of processes, of necessity. It hugs the easy way of damning those whom it cannot understand, of excluding those who look different, and it salves its conscience with a self-draped cloak of righteousness.

Am I damning my native land? No; for I, too, share these faults of character! And I really do not

> think that America, adolescent and cocksure, a stranger to suffering and travail, an enemy of passion and sacrifice, is ready to probe into its most fundamental beliefs.
>
> Richard Wright, *Black Boy*

Christians need support in our country and around the world. Their religious liberty is at stake. Obama has been horrible. I will be great.

Facebook post, September 20, 2015

> How dismal it is to see present day Americans yearning for the very orthodoxy that their country was founded to escape.
>
> Christopher Hitchens

Almost as bad as they have ever been in the history of the country.

Answering the question "How would you describe race relations in 2015 in Obama's America?," The Economist interview, September 3, 2015

Segregation in the South is honest, open and aboveboard. Of the two systems, or styles of segregation, the Northern and the Southern, there is no doubt whatever in my mind which is the better.

Strom Thurmond

Trump, the Man and the Ego

From a young age, Trump's only priority has been Donald Trump. Although he was not alone among young men of the Vietnam era in seeking draft deferments, Donald Trump sought and received four, including one for medical reasons, which let him sit out a war.

Since then, every maneuver, every step in Donald Trump's life has been focused on enriching and bettering himself. Trump famously said of his first wife, Ivana, in 1990, "I would never buy Ivana any decent jewels or pictures. Why give her negotiable assets?" Trump claims to have given millions of dollars to charity, but an investigation by *The Washington Post* found that Trump had donated nothing to charity in the five years leading up to the election. Trump looks after Trump. Since 2008, Trump has given none of his own money to his Trump Foundation.

Looking after Trump involves accumulating personal wealth and sitting on the altar of greed, but it also involves not doing anything that he doesn't care to do, such as child-rearing. In 2005, Trump told Howard Stern, "'Cause I like kids. I mean, I won't do anything to take care of them. I'll supply funds and she'll take care of the kids. It's not like I'm gonna be walking the kids down Central Park."

Trump is a narcissist and bully. He is self-centered, and yet his ego is made of fragile egg shells. He blocks people on Twitter who insult him or hurt his feelings. Novelist Stephen King is one of those whom Trump has blocked.

And of course, he's a habitual liar. *The New York Times*[3], in its ever-expanding list of President Trump's verified lies, points out that he lied daily during his first forty days in office.

Trump extended his ego through fictitious spokesmen John Miller and John Barron for three decades, starting in the 1970s. Trump would call reporters claiming to be Miller or Barron and extol Donald Trump's achievements.

On July 26, 2017, Trump announced a new policy: Transgender people would no longer be allowed to serve in the military. Trump's announcement was three tweets long, starting with this one: "After consultation with my Generals and military experts, please be advised that the United States Government will not accept or allow . . ."

Trump waited nine minutes to complete the tweet and reveal that this was about transgender members of the military. Anyone reading Trump's incomplete tweet—and

3. https://www.nytimes.com/interactive/2017/06/23/opinion/trumps-lies.html

I was one of them—was sweating. Was Trump announcing a military action against another country? Was Trump going to complete the sentence with, ". . . ourselves to be threatened by North Korea, so we have taken preemptive action and launched missiles against Pyongyang."

Only Trump knows if he deliberately decided to cause global anxiety, or if this was just really, really bad judgment. Either way, this shows how thoughtless Trump is toward others. Toward the entire world.

One of the mainstays of horror fiction is the monster that consumes humans.

Some monsters eat our physical parts, like vampires who drink blood, or the salt monster in the first Star Trek episode, which eats people's salt and kills them.

Then, there are the monsters that need to consume people's emotions to live. Dementors in Harry Potter feed on human happiness. The parasite in Vincent Price's 1959 horror movie, *The Tingler*, lives off fear; this is the parasite that makes our spines tingle when we're suddenly scared.

Now we have Donald Trump, who must consume people's veneration to survive. Veneration is as necessary to Trump as food and water are for regular humans.

Sorry losers and haters, but my I.Q. is one of the highest—and you all know it! Please don't feel so stupid or insecure, it's not your fault.

Twitter, May 9 2013

> The difference between stupidity and genius is that genius has its limits.
>
> Albert Einstein

With the exception of the late, great Abraham Lincoln, I can be more presidential than any president that's ever held this office.

Speech in Youngstown, Ohio, July 25, 2017

> I never did give them hell. I just told the truth, and they thought it was hell.
>
> Harry Truman

The global warming we should be worried about is the global warming caused by NUCLEAR WEAPONS in the hands of crazy or incompetent leaders!

Tweet, May 8 2014

> We must, I believe, start teaching our children the sanity of nonviolence much earlier.
>
> Alice Walker

I'm having a good time, but Howard, you know the one negative: It's very, very dangerous out there . . . It's Vietnam. It is very dangerous. So I'm very, very careful.

Howard Stern show May 7, 1998, comparing the risk of contracting a sexually transmitted disease with serving in Vietnam. Trump did not serve in the military, having been granted five deferments.

> Happiness is a risk. If you're not a little scared, then you're not doing it right.
>
> Sarah Addison Allen, *The Peach Keeper*

I get it when I need it . . . I'm, like, a smart person. I don't have to be told the same thing in the same words every single day for the next eight years. I don't need that.

Trump explaining why he doesn't need daily intelligence briefings, Fox News, December 11, 2016. As president, "Donald Trump likes his daily intelligence briefings to be short and with 'killer graphics,' The Washington Post *reported on Monday," writes Business Insider.*

> I can calculate the motion of heavenly bodies but not the madness of people.
>
> Isaac Newton

Every single president on Mount Rushmore . . . Now here's what I do, I'd ask whether or not you think I will one day on Mount Rushmore. But here's the problem. If I did it joking, totally joking, having fun, the fake news media will say "he believes he belongs on Mount Rushmore." So I won't say it, all right?

Speech in Youngstown, Ohio, July 25, 2017

> Huxley: "Tell me something Bryce, do you know the difference between a Jersey, a Guernsey, a Holstein, and an Ayershire?"
>
> Bryce: "No."
>
> Huxley: "Seabags Brown does."
>
> Bryce: "I don't see what that has to do . . ."
>
> Huxley: "What do you know about Gaelic history?"
>
> Bryce: "Not much."

Huxley: "Then why don't you sit down one day with Gunner McQuade. He is an expert. Speaks the language, too."

Bryce: "I don't . . ."

Huxley: " What do you know about astronomy?"

Bryce: "A little."

Huxley: "Discuss it with Wellman, he held a fellowship."

Bryce: "This is most puzzling."

Huxley: "What about Homer, ever read Homer?"

Bryce: "Of course I've read Homer."

Huxley: "In the original Greek?"

Bryce: "No."

Huxley: "Then chat with Pfc. Hodgkiss. Loves to read the ancient Greek."

Bryce: "Would you kindly get to the point?"

Huxley: "The point is this, Bryce. What makes you think you are so goddam superior? Who gave you the bright idea that you had a corner on the world's knowledge? There are privates in this battalion who can piss more brains down a slit trench then you'll ever have. You're the most pretentious, egotistical individual I've ever encountered. Your superiority complex reeks. I've seen the way you treat men, like a big strutting peacock. Why, you've had them do everything but wipe your ass."

Leon Uris, *Battle Cry*

I'm also honored to have the greatest temperament that anybody has.

November 3, 2016

> You never really learn much from hearing yourself speak.
>
> George Clooney

I love covers, especially, it would be an honour, especially if you write well. If it's a cover where you write badly, that's even okay. You have a great magazine.

The Economist *interview, September 3, 2015, responding to being told that his interview would be a cover story in* The Economist.

> Better to remain silent and be thought a fool than to speak and to remove all doubt.
>
> Abraham Lincoln

This is going to kill me. I am the world's greatest person that does not want to let people into the country. And now I am agreeing to take 2,000 people.

Trump on the phone with Australian Prime Minister Malcolm Turnbull, pleading with the prime minister to reverse the agreement by which America would accept refugees from Australia, January 2017. As is often the case, Trump matters more to Trump than America does.

> With enough courage, you can do without a reputation.
>
> Margaret Mitchell

I'm strongly into the Bible. I'm strongly into God and religion. I'm pro-life and different things.

The Economist *interview, September 3, 2015*

> People in Hollywood are not show men, they're maintenance men, pandering to what they think their audiences want.
>
> Terry Gilliam

We love the Bible. That's the book. It's the best. We love *The Art of the Deal*, but the Bible is far far far superior, right?

Council Bluffs, Iowa, December 2015

> Not only is the Bible better than *The Art of the Deal*, it's also the opposite.
>
> Seth Meyers, August 1, 2017

I think the only difference between me and the other candidates is that I'm more honest and my women are more beautiful.

Quoted in 1999 interview with The New York Times *columnist Maureen Dowd. Trump was considering running for president in 2000.*

> Be yourself; everyone else is already taken.
>
> Oscar Wilde

I have the world's greatest memory. It's one thing everyone agrees on.

November 24, 2015

> The scenes aired Monday on Fox News as President Trump landed at Joint Base Andrews airfield. He is seen stepping off the plane and waving to a gathered crowd. However, when he reaches the bottom of the steps, he seems to miss his ride—parked directly in front of the jet—and walks off in a different direction. Maybe, like his alternative facts, he just prefers alternative routes? Trump is then redirected to his awaiting car by an aide.
>
> *Newsweek*, July 5, 2017

I am willing to say that we will work it out, but that means it will come out in the wash and that is okay. But you cannot say anymore that the United States is going to pay for the wall . . . [M]y position has been and will continue to be very firm saying that Mexico cannot pay for that wall . . . But you cannot say to that to the press. The press is going to go with that and I cannot live with that.

Donald Trump's phone call with Mexican President Enrique Peña, January 27, 2017. In this phone call Trump reveals his innermost fear and reason why "the wall" must go forward and Mexico must pay: If Trump's plans are upset, he will become a laughingstock. Trump's greatest worry is not doing what's best for America; it's avoiding personal humiliation.

> Oh, humiliation is poisonous. It's one of the deepest pains of being human.
>
> Pierce Brosnan

I know more about ISIS than the generals do, believe me. I would bomb the shit out of them.

November 13, 2015

> Great minds are always feared by lesser minds.
>
> Dan Brown, *The Lost Symbol*

Do you notice when I go on and I'll put out like a tweet or a couple of tweets, "He's in a Twitter storm again." I don't do Twitter storms.

In Phoenix, Arizona, August 22, 2017, at a campaign-style rally. It's called a "tweetstorm," and yes, Trump obviously does.

> Being a practiced liar doesn't mean you have a powerful imagination. Many good liars have no imagination at all; it's that which gives their lies such wide-eyed conviction.
>
> Philip Pullman, *The Golden Compass*

I predicted Osama bin Laden. In my book, I predicted terrorism. Because I can feel it, like I feel a good location, okay?

Nashville, Tennessee, November 16, 2015

> My bullshit meter is reading that as "false."
>
> Charlaine Harris, *Dead as a Doornail*

In the old days when you wanted to attack, you had a courier with armed guards and you'd have an envelope and you'd give it to the general. Now you send it to the general and you have no idea how many people are watching and reading. They're hacking your messages. I think [General Douglas] MacArthur would not like the whole concept of computers.

Hugh Hewitt interview, October 22, 2015. Trump, calling himself "modern presidential" because he tweets, has on more than one occasion shown both disdain for and confusion about technology.

> Once you have an innovation culture, even those who are not scientists or engineers—poets, actors, journalists—they, as communities, embrace the meaning of what it is to be scientifically literate. They embrace the concept of an innovation culture. They vote in ways that promote it. They don't fight science and they don't fight technology.
>
> Neil deGrasse Tyson

"I think apologizing's a great thing, but you have to be wrong. I will absolutely apologize, sometime in the hopefully distant future, if I'm ever wrong."

The Tonight Show with Jimmy Fallon, *September 2015*

> The best of us must sometimes eat our words.
>
> J.K. Rowling

I'm a very stable person. I'm so stable you wouldn't believe it.

Time Magazine *interview, July 2016*

> Together with open conversations and greater understanding, we can ensure that attitudes for mental health change and children receive the support they deserve.
>
> Kate Middleton

I do a book called *The Art of the Deal.* It's probably the number one selling business book of all time. I go to the Wharton School of Finance. I was a good student in the hardest school where there was to get into. . . .

And then they say, "Oh, he's not qualified," and they take some dope who becomes a senator, who doesn't have—who's nothing, and he's qualified to be on the stage, but Trump isn't qualified? Give me a break.

Responding to a question about whether he's qualified to be a candidate for president, MSNBC interview, June 18, 2015

> I put lipstick on a pig. I feel a deep sense of remorse that I contributed to presenting Trump in a way that brought him wider attention and made him more appealing than he is.
>
> Tony Schwartz, ghostwriter for *The Art of the Deal*, quoted in the *The New Yorker*, July 25, 2016

I think Ronald Reagan liked me a lot more than he liked a lot of other people.

Speech, North Charleston, South Carolina, September 23, 2015

> On the throne of the world, any delusion can become fact.
>
> Gore Vidal, *Julian*

I'm a solid, stable person. I am a man of great achievement. I win, Maureen, I always win. Knock on wood, I win. It's what I do. I beat people. I win.

Interview with Maureen Dowd, The New York Times, *August 15, 2015*

> "A man's greatest pleasure is to defeat his enemies, to drive them before him, to take from them that which they possessed, to see those whom they cherished in tears, to ride their horses, and to hold their wives and daughters in his arms."
>
> Genghis Khan

I like a lot of books. I like reading books. I don't have the time to read very much now in terms of books, but I like reading them.

January 2017. Trump doesn't read books.

> A book is the most effective weapon against intolerance and ignorance.
>
> Lyndon Baines Johnson

Would you rather have experience or talent? I'll take talent every time. That's not to knock experience, and I think I have both.

Time Magazine *interview, July 2016*

> Talent is a gift, but character is a choice.
>
> John C. Maxwell

Sometimes you need conflict in order to come up with a solution. Through weakness, oftentimes, you can't make the right sort of settlement, so I'm aggressive, but I also get things done, and in the end, everybody likes me.

Rolling Stone *magazine interview, May 26, 2011*

> "I am in love with you," I responded.
>
> He laughed the most beguiling and gentle laugh.
>
> "Of course you are," he replied. "I understand perfectly because I'm in love with myself. The fact that I'm not transfixed in front of the nearest mirror takes a great deal of self-control."
>
> It was my turn to laugh.
>
> Anne Rice, *Blackwood Farm*

When you talk about the nuclear button, the ones I'm worried about are the other people on the other side that have the nuclear. But don't worry about me.

Sean Hannity interview, Fox News, June 17, 2015

There's never been a true war that wasn't fought between two sets of people who were certain they were in the right. The really dangerous people believe they are doing whatever they are doing solely and only because it is without question the right thing to do. And that is what makes them dangerous.

Neil Gaiman, *American Gods*

When somebody challenges you unfairly, fight back—be brutal, be tough—don't take it. It is always important to WIN!

Tweet, June 27, 2015

I've missed more than 9,000 shots in my career. I've lost almost 300 games. Twenty-sixtimes, I've been trusted to take the game winning shot and missed. I've failed over and over and over again in my life. And that is why I succeed.

Michael Jordan

You know the funny thing, I don't get along with rich people. I get along with the middle class and the poor people better than I get along with the rich people.

New Hampshire, February 8, 2016

> I'm not upset that you lied to me, I'm upset that from now on I can't believe you.
>
> Friedrich Nietzsche

Jeff Sessions takes the job, gets into the job, recuses himself. I then have—which, frankly, I think is very unfair to the president. How do you take a job and then recuse yourself? If he would have recused himself before the job, I would have said, "Thanks, Jeff, but I can't, you know, I'm not going to take you." It's extremely unfair, and that's a mild word, to the president. So he recuses himself. I then end up with a second man, who's a deputy.

The New York Times *interview, July 19, 2017*

> When problems arise, you will usually find two types of people: whiners and winners. Whiners obstruct progress; they spend hours complaining about this point or that, without offering positive solutions. Winners acknowledge the existence of the problem, but they try to offer practical ideas

> that can help resolve the matter in a manner that is satisfactory to both parties.
>
> George Foreman

My net worth fluctuates, and it goes up and down with the markets and with attitudes and with feelings, even my own feelings, but I try. . . . Yes, even my own feelings, as to where the world is, where the world is going, and that can change rapidly from day to day.

Trump, during a legal deposition, answering a question about his net worth, December 2007

> I'm sorry to say that the subject I most disliked was mathematics. I have thought about it. I think the reason was that mathematics leaves no room for argument. If you made a mistake, that was all there was to it.
>
> Malcolm X

I have a very simple rule when it comes to management: hire the best people from your competitors, pay them more than they were earning, and give them bonuses and incentives based on their performance. That's how you build a first-class operation.

The Art of the Deal

> *Headline: Help wanted: Why Republicans won't work for the Trump administration*
>
> Republicans say they are turning down job offers to work for a chief executive whose volatile temperament makes them nervous. They are asking head-hunters if their reputations could suffer permanent damage, according to 27 people The Washington Post interviewed to assess what is becoming a debilitating factor in recruiting political appointees.
>
> The Washington Post, June 17, 2017

The other night, I was surprised when I heard a couple of my friends—my friends—they really were and are. They might not be very much longer, but that's okay.

Talking about senators Mike Lee (R-Utah) and Jerry Moran (R-Kansas), who announced they were voting against the Senate healthcare plan Trump supported, July 19, 2017

> Friendship marks a life even more deeply than love. Love risks degenerating into obsession, friendship is never anything but sharing.
>
> Elie Wiesel

I really think I am a nice person.

The Economist *interview, September 3, 2015*

> Crocodiles are easy. They try to kill and eat you. People are harder. Sometimes they pretend to be your friend first.
>
> Steve Irwin

I have a great temperament. My temperament is very good, very calm.

Presidential debate, September 15, 2016

> You can't get away from yourself by moving from one place to another.
>
> Ernest Hemingway, *The Sun Also Rises*

I tend to be right. I'm an instinctual person, I happen to be a person that knows how life works.

Time Magazine *interview, March, 2017*

> At most, recognizing that our history was inspired by many tales we now recognize as false should make us alert, ready to call to constantly into question the very tale we believe true, because the criterion of the wisdom of the community is based on constant awareness of the fallibility of our learning.
>
> Umberto Eco

He referred to my hands, if they're small, something else must be small. I guarantee you there's no problem. I guarantee it.

Replying to a joking remark made by Senator Mark Rubio during the GOP debate, March 3, 2016

> The problem is God gave man a brain and a penis and only enough blood to run one at a time.
>
> Robin Williams

People understand that the house in Florida is business. I use it very seldom. I could be happy living in a studio apartment.

Playboy *magazine interview, March 1, 1990*

Honesty is a rare commodity in a palace, and that is why so many fairy-tale marriages end up on the rocks.

Garrison Keillor

I think I've made a lot of sacrifices. I work very, very hard. I've created thousands and thousands of jobs, tens of thousands of jobs, built great structures. I've had tremendous success. I think I've done a lot.

ABC interview, July 30, 2016, answering the question, "What sacrifices have you made?"

During my lifetime I have dedicated myself to this struggle of the African people. I have fought against white domination, and I have fought against black domination. I have cherished the ideal of a democratic and free society in which all persons live together in harmony and with equal opportunities. It is an ideal which I hope to live

> for and to achieve. But if needs be, it is an ideal for which I am prepared to die.
>
> Nelson Mandela

A lot of the people have said that, some people said it was the single best speech ever made in that chamber.

Talking about his first address to Congress in an interview with the Associated Press, April 22, 2017

> The worst disease which can afflict executives in their work is not, as popularly supposed, alcoholism; it's egotism.
>
> Robert Frost

I don't like to lie, no. I don't like to lie, no. It's something that—it's not something that I would like to be doing.

Interview, January 2017

> Donald Trump made 21 false claims last week, has said 358 false things as president so far.
>
> *Toronto Star*, July 5, 2017

It's the highest for *Deface the Nation* since the World Trade Center. Since the World Trade Center came down. It's a tremendous advantage.

Trump claiming that his appearance on Face the Nation *earned that show its highest rating since 9-11, Associated Press interview, April 22, 2017*

> "Not everything is about you," Clary said furiously.
>
> "Possibly," Jace said, "but you do have to admit that the majority of things are."
>
> Cassandra Clare, *City of Glass*

40 Wall Street actually was the second-tallest building in downtown Manhattan. And now it's the tallest.

Trump bragging how his building, 40 Wall Street, became the tallest building in New York after the Twin Towers were destroyed on 9/11. (He was wrong about that, too: 70 Pine Street is taller.)

> Dallas hit a chord back in the late Seventies and Eighties because it was the age of greed: here you have this unapologetic character who is mean and nasty and ruthless and does it all with an evil grin. I think people related to JR back then because we all have someone we know exactly like him. Everyone in the world knows a JR.
>
> Larry Hagman, actor

My experience yesterday in Poland was a great one. Thank you to everyone, including the haters, for the great reviews of the speech!

Tweet, July 7, 2017

> For twenty-three years I've been dying to tell you what I thought of you! And now—well, being a Christian woman, I can't say it.
>
> Auntie Em from *The Wizard of Oz*, 1939

One of my greatest passions is making deals. I love to make the big score and to make the big deal. I love to crush the other side and take the benefits. Why? Because there is nothing greater. For me it is even better than sex, and I love sex. But when you hit, when the deals are going your way, it is the greatest feeling! You hear lots of people say that a great deal is when both sides win. That is a bunch of crap. In a great deal you win—not the other side. You crush the opponent and come away with something better for yourself. In negotiations I love to go for the complete win. That is why I have made so many good deals.

Think Big, *2008*

> Until he extends the circle of his compassion to all living things, man will not himself find peace.
>
> Albert Schweitzer

You know we've gotten billions of dollars more in NATO than that we're getting. All because of me. I mean it's not like a bragging thing, I'm just saying. If Hillary Clinton would have gotten in, she wouldn't even know that we're getting screwed by everybody.

Time Magazine *interview, May 11, 2017*

> There are all kinds of stupid people that annoy me but what annoys me most is a lazy argument.
>
> Christopher Hitchens

I work out on occasion. As little as possible.

1997 interview

> A bear, however hard he tries, grows tubby without exercise.
>
> A.A. Milne, *Winnie-the-Pooh*

I like kids. I mean, I won't do anything to take care of them. I'll supply funds, and she'll take care of the kids.

Interview with Howard Stern, 2005

> I love every minute of fatherhood, staying up all night, changing nappies, kids crying, I find it really funny and inspiring. It connects you to the world in a new way.
>
> Elton John

I will be the greatest jobs president that God ever created.

Formally announcing his candidacy for president, June 16, 2015

> No experience of the failure of his policy could shake his belief in its essential excellence.
>
> Barbara Tuchman, *The March of Folly*

The fundamental question of our time is whether the West has the will to survive.

Warsaw, Poland, July 6, 2017

> Turning and turning in the widening gyre
> The falcon cannot hear the falconer;
> Things fall apart; the centre cannot hold;
> Mere anarchy is loosed upon the world,

> The blood-dimmed tide is loosed, and everywhere
> The ceremony of innocence is drowned;
> The best lack all conviction, while the worst
> Are full of passionate intensity.
>
> W.B. Yeats, "The Second Coming," excerpt

I like bullets or I like as little as possible. I don't need, you know, 200-page reports on something that can be handled on a page. That I can tell you.

On how he likes to digest information, January, 2017. Foreign Policy *magazine reported on May 15, 2017: "NATO is scrambling to tailor its upcoming meeting to avoid taxing President Donald Trump's notoriously short attention span. The alliance is telling heads of state to limit talks to two to four minutes at a time during the discussion."*

> The more that you read, the more things you will know. The more that you learn, the more places you'll go.
>
> Dr. Seuss, *I Can Read With My Eyes Shut!*

I don't have a racist bone in my body.

Entertainment Tonight, *July 1, 2015*

> Things like racism are institutionalized. You might not know any bigots. You feel like, "Well I don't hate black people so I'm not a racist," but you benefit from racism. Just by the merit, the color of your skin. The opportunities that you have, you're privileged in ways that you might not even realize because you haven't been deprived of certain things. We need to talk about these things in order for them to change.
>
> Dave Chappelle

I'm not a big shorts person. Personally, I hate to see men's legs on the golf course.

Donald Trump

> What most people don't understand is that UFOs are on a cosmic tourist route. That's why they're always seen in Arizona, Scotland, and New Mexico. Another thing to consider is that all three of those destinations are good places to play golf. So there's possibly some connection between aliens and golf.
>
> Alice Cooper

I'm dealing with a man, I think I like him a lot. I think he likes me a lot. We were supposed to meet for ten minutes and they go to 40-person meetings, OK, in Mar-a-Lago, in Palm Beach. And the ten minutes turned out to be three hours, alone, the two of us. The next day it was supposed to be ten minutes and then we go to our 40-person meeting. That, too, he was, no . . . because you guys were waiting for a long time. That ten-minute meeting turned out to be three hours. Dinner turned out to be three hours. I mean, he's a great guy.

Talking about China's President Xi Jinping, The Economist *interview, May 11, 2017*

> I find comfort in the fact that the longer I'm in politics the less nourishing popularity becomes, that striving for power and rank and fame seems to betray a poverty of ambition, and that I am answerable mainly to the steady gaze of my own conscience.
>
> Barack Obama, *The Audacity of Hope: Thoughts on Reclaiming the American Dream*

Everything I've done virtually has been a tremendous success.

Presidential debate, September 16, 2015

> The *New York Times* rates 61 of Donald Trump's business deals, concludes 40% failed. . . .
>
> The reporters concluded that 24 of those deals failed, 16 had problems, and 21 were successes. They didn't outline the methodology that led them to these conclusions. Some of the projects The *Times* categorizes as unsuccessful may have earned Trump hefty sums (like Trump Taj Mahal in Atlantic City, for example), as he pointed out in an interview for the story.
>
> Business Insider, October 6, 2016

My wife says I'm the biggest star in the world. But she might just be saying that because she's intelligent.

GQ *interview, 2009*

> I become quite melancholy and deeply grieved to see men behave to each other as they do. Everywhere I find nothing but base flattery, injustice, self-interest, deceit and roguery. I cannot bear it any longer; I'm furious; and my intention is to break with all mankind.
>
> Molière, *The Misanthrope*

My use of social media is not Presidential—it's MODERN DAY PRESIDENTIAL. Make America Great Again!

Tweet, July 2, 2017

> Distracted from distraction by distraction.
>
> T.S. Eliot

Which is true, actually, I actually have low blood pressure, can you believe it? Can you believe it? I have like 100 over something. The doctor said, "Man, you have the blood pressure of a great, great, athlete who is 20 years old. 110, I like that, because I like being a great athlete."

Campaign rally in Waterbury, Connecticut, April 23, 2016

> When a liar became too skilled at deception, he could lose the ability to discern truth, and could himself be more easily deceived.
>
> Dean Koontz, *Velocity*

I feel like a supermodel except, like, times 10, okay? It's true. I'm a supermodel.

Campaign rally, Arizona, June 18, 2016

> Egotist, *n.* A person of low taste, more interested in himself than in me.
>
> Ambrose Bierce, *The Unabridged Devil's Dictionary*

They won't even give him stairs, proper stairs to get out of the airplane. You see that? They have pictures of other leaders who are . . . coming down with a beautiful red carpet. And Obama is coming down a metal staircase. I've got to tell you, if that were me, I would say, "You know what, folks, I respect you a lot but close the doors, let's get out of here." It's a sign of such disrespect.

Talking about how the wrong stairs were brought to Air Force One when President Obama landed in China at a meeting with labor leaders in Brook Park, Ohio, September 5, 2016

> I believe that the mind can be permanently profaned by the habit of attending to trivial things.
>
> Henry David Thoreau

It's never different. I think it's never different. It's always the same. You have to know your subject. And that would be the misconception of misconceptions for that. I mean, it's not that I—look, I always had health care for my company. But it's not that I—it was just something that wasn't high on my list. I had people that negotiated for my company.

But in a short period of time I understood everything there was to know about health care. And we did the right negotiating, and actually it's a very interesting subject.

Time Magazine *interview, May 11, 2017*

> The biggest fool is the one who thinks he knows it all.
>
> Piers Anthony

I discovered, for the first time but not the last, that politicians don't care too much what things cost. It's not their money.

The Art of the Deal

> Donald Trump's Mar-a-Lago trips cost taxpayers estimated $20m in 100 days—Obama's cost $97m in 8 years.
>
> *The Independent* (UK), April 29, 2017

The final key to the way I promote is bravado. I play to people's fantasies. People may not always think big themselves. but they can get very excited by those who do. That is why a little hyperbole never hurts. People want to believe that something is the biggest, the greatest and the most spectacular.

Trump, The Art of the Deal

> Teddy said it was a hat,/ So I put it on. Now Dad is saying, "Where the heck's the toilet plunger gone?"
>
> Shel Silverstein

I built a phenomenal business with incredible, iconic assets. And I may be an entertainer, because I've had tremendous success with No. 1 bestsellers all over the place.

Republican Party primary debate, September 16, 2015

> Dana Barrett: You know, you don't act like a scientist.
>
> Dr. Peter Venkman: They're usually pretty stiff.
>
> Dana Barrett: You're more like a game show host.
>
> *Ghostbusters,* 1984

The happiest people I know are those people who have great families and real values. I've seen it. I know it. People who have a loving spouse and have children they really love are happy people. Religion also plays a very large factor in happiness. People who have God in their lives receive a tremendous amount of joy and satisfaction from their faith.

Crippled America

> In modern life nothing produces such an effect as a good platitude. It makes the whole world kin.
>
> Oscar Wilde

You do your job, you keep your job. Do it well, you get a better job.

Crippled America

> I was raised by a single mom who had to put herself through school while looking after two kids. And she worked hard every day and made a lot of sacrifices to make sure we got everything we needed. My grandmother, she started off as a secretary in a bank. She never got a college education, even though she was smart as a whip. And she worked her way up to become a vice president of a local bank, but she hit the glass ceiling. She

> trained people who would end up becoming her bosses during the course of her career.
>
> Barack Obama

I think people are shocked when they find out that I am a Christian, that I am a religious person. . . . I go to church, I love God, and I love having a relationship with him.

Trump, Crippled America

> But people love a hypocrite, you know—they recognize one of their own, and it always feels so good when someone gets caught with his pants down and his dick up and it isn't you.
>
> Stephen King, *The Green Mile*

People are surprised to learn that I put in 12-hour working days. For me, that's the norm, not the exception. To remain successful, I have to be persistent and work hard; I work long hours to get everything done. If you usually work a 40-hour week and then add on another 20 hours a week for a few weeks, you'll be surprised at how much more you can accomplish. Productive people accomplish more for a reason—they work long and hard.

Trump 101, *2006*

That the crowd always likes a holiday is a common saying, but when the whole year becomes one long holiday, and nobody has time for attending to his business, and pleasure becomes compulsory, then it is a different matter.

Robert Graves, *I, Claudius*

Russia and the Time of Troubles

The history of Donald Trump's involvement with Russia will be written, just as the history of Watergate was written. Whatever Trump's involvement with Russia is, one thing's certain: He wants to hide it and confuse people about it and do everything in his power to keep people from uncovering his Russia connections. But the truth is a not only a powerful force; it is like steel, and the world around it is a super magnet.

Trump's triad of tools—deny, thwart, and distract—thinned and weakened about the tenth time he called the investigation into Russia's interference with the U.S. presidential election a "witch hunt." Calling the investigation a "witch hunt" wasn't clever in the first place, and the expression quickly became tedious and trite.

In November 2013, Trump told NBC, "I do have a relationship [with Putin] and I can tell you that he's very interested in what we're doing here today." In March 2014, Trump insisted, "I was in Moscow a couple months ago, I own the Miss Universe pageant, and they treated me so great. Putin even sent me a present, beautiful present, with a beautiful note." Next year in May Trump said, "I was in Moscow recently. And I spoke indirectly—and directly—with President Putin, who could not have been nicer."

In November 2015, Trump crowed, "As far as the Ukraine is concerned, and you could Syria—as far as Syria, I like—if Putin wants to go in, and I got to know him very well because we were both on '60 Minutes,' we were stablemates, and we did very well that night. But, you know that."

Okay. It's settled then. Trump knew Putin before his first public meeting with the Russian president at the G20 Summit in July 2017. Wait a second. During the campaign, in July 2016, Trump slammed on the brakes, turned his car around, and claimed just the opposite: "I never met Putin, I don't know who Putin is. He said one nice thing about me. He said I'm a genius. I said thank you very much to the newspaper and that was the end of it. I never met Putin." In an ABC interview the following month, Trump claimed, "I have no relationship to—with him. I have no relationship with him." When pressed by George Stephanopoulos about whether he'd met Putin, Trump did his absolute best not to answer the question: "I have no relationship with Putin. I don't think I've ever met him. I never met him. I don't think I've ever met him. . . . I don't know what it means by having a relationship. I mean he was saying very good things about me, but I don't have a relationship with him. I didn't meet him.

I haven't spent time with him. I didn't have dinner with him. I didn't go hiking with him."

Sure sounds like lying.

During the G20 Summit in July 2017, Trump had an off-the-books meeting with Vladimir Putin. No American advisors accompanied Trump. The only translator was a Russian, putting the American president at a significant disadvantage with his Russian counterpart. When asked what they talked about, Trump said, "I actually talked about Russian adoption with him, which is interesting because it was a part of the conversation that [Donald Trump Jr.] had in that meeting." By now, the world knows that "Russian adoption" is code for a United States law, the Magnitsky Act, which freezes certain assets and imposes visa restrictions on Russians thought to have committed human rights violations. Adoptions, my ass.

I am being investigated for firing the FBI Director by the man who told me to fire the FBI Director! Witch Hunt

Tweet, June 16, 2017. "Witch hunt" became one of Trump's most popular clichés during the Russia investigation.

> Let me never fall into the vulgar mistake of dreaming that I am persecuted whenever I am contradicted.
>
> Ralph Waldo Emerson, *Emerson in His Journals*

I just fired the head of the F.B.I. He was crazy, a real nut job. I faced great pressure because of Russia. That's taken off.

Trump explaining to Russian officials at the White House why he fired FBI Director James Comey.

> Mary wished to say something very sensible, but knew not how.
>
> Jane Austen, *Pride and Prejudice*

Russian officials must be laughing at the U.S. & how a lame excuse for why the Dems lost the election has taken over the Fake News.

Tweet, May 30, 2017. Russian officials likely laughed when Trump inadvertently revealed highly classified information to the Russian foreign minister during a May 10, 2017 meeting. Trump revealed code-word-level information the United States had received from Israel about a planned ISIS attack. From this revelation, Russia could learn about intelligence sources and other information.

> "It was a mistake," you said. But the cruel thing was, it felt like the mistake was mine, for trusting you."
>
> David Levithan, *The Lover's Dictionary*

This is the single greatest witch hunt of a politician in American history!

Tweet about the investigation into possible collusion between Russia and the Trump campaign, May 17, 2017

> I want the light of God, I want the sweet love of Jesus! I danced for the Devil; I saw him, I wrote in his book; I go back to Jesus; I kiss His hand. I saw Sarah Good with the Devil! I saw Goody Osburn

> with the Devil! I saw Bridget Bishop with the Devil!
>
> Abigail Williams confessing to be a witch in Arthur Miller's *The Crucible*

We just left Moscow. [Putin] could not have been nicer. He was so nice and so everything. But you have to give him credit that what he's doing for that country in terms of their world prestige is very strong. . . .

Well, [Putin's] done an amazing job of taking the mantle. And he's taken it away from the President, and you look at what he's doing. And so smart. When you see the riots in a country because they're hurting the Russians, okay, 'We'll go and take it over.' And he really goes step by step by step, and you have to give him a lot of credit.

About Putin and Putin's invasion of Crimea, April 12, 2014

> Who ever heard of a Martian not invading? Who!
>
> Ray Bradbury, *The Concrete Mixer*

You know what? I don't even think of pardons. Here's why, nobody did anything wrong. Look at Jared, everybody—we do appreciate the editorial—but everybody said Jared Kushner. Jared's a very private person. He doesn't get out.

I mean, maybe it's good or maybe it's bad what I do, but at least people know how I feel. Jared's this really nice, smart guy, who'd love to see peace in the Middle East and in Israel, okay?

Answering a question during a Wall Street Journal *interview about pardons and his son-in-law, Jared Kushner, July 25, 2017*

> Fact is, all lies, all evil deeds, they stink. You can cover them up for a while, but they don't go away.
>
> Dalton Russell, in the movie *Inside Man*, 2016

The Russia story is a total fabrication. It's just an excuse for the greatest loss in the history of American politics, that's all it is.

It just makes them feel better when they have nothing else to talk about. What the prosecutors should be looking at are Hillary Clinton's 33,000 deleted emails.

And they should be looking at the paid Russian speeches. And the owned Russian companies. Or let them look at the uranium she sold that is now in the hands of very angry Russians. Most people know there were no Russians in our campaign, there never were.

West Virginia campaign-style speech, August 3, 2017. Trump gave this speech on the day the press reported that a grand jury is now involved in investigating Trump's campaign and Russia.

> I try to deny myself any illusions or delusions, and I think that this perhaps entitles me to try and deny the same to others, at least as long as they refuse to keep their fantasies to themselves.
>
> Christopher Hitchens, *Hitch-22: A Memoir*

When Nixon came along [inaudible] was pretty brutal, and out of courtesy, the FBI started reporting to the Department of Justice. But there was nothing official, there was nothing from Congress. There was nothing—anything. But the FBI person really reports directly to the president of the United States, which is interesting.

The New York Times *interview, July 19, 2017. The FBI director reports to the attorney general, not to the president.*

> I always tell the truth. Even when I lie.
>
> Al Pacino

When I went to Russia with the Miss Universe pageant, [Putin] contacted me and was so nice. I mean, the Russian people were so fantastic to us. I'll just say this, they are doing—they're outsmarting us at many turns, as we all understand. I mean, their leaders are, whether you call them smarter or more cunning or whatever, but they're outsmarting us. If you look at Syria or other places, they're outsmarting us.

Fox and Friends, *February 10, 2014*

> *Quand celui à qui l'on parle ne comprend pas et celui qui parle ne se comprend pas, c'est de la métaphysique.*
>
> When the person to whom one is speaking does not understand, and he who speaks does not understand himself, that is metaphysics.
>
> Voltaire

Does anybody really think Hillary Clinton would be tougher on Russia than Donald Trump?

February 2017

> "Kremlin Names Trump Employee of the Month"
>
> Andy Borowitz, *New Yorker*, December 30, 2016. Andy Borowitz is the *New Yorker*'s satirist.

HillaryClinton can illegally get the questions to the Debate & delete 33,000 emails but my son Don is being scorned by the Fake News Media?

Tweet, July 16, 2017. (HillaryClinton was written as one word.) Trump frequently tried to deflect the Russia investigation by saying that Hillary Clinton should be investigated, long after the campaign ended.

> Well, the first thing we do is take our brain out and put it in a drawer. Stick it somewhere and let it tantrum until it wears itself out. You may still hear the brain and all the shitty things it is saying to you, but it will be muffled, and just the fact that it is not in your head anymore will make things seem clearer.
>
> Amy Poehler

So why aren't the Committees and investigators, and of course our beleaguered A.G., looking into Crooked Hillarys crimes & Russia relations?

Tweet, July 24, 2017

> "Don't be so damned patronizing. Your performance so far has been a little less than dazzling."
>
> "I didn't mean no harm," I said and kissed her. "That a new dress?"
>
> "Ah! Changing the subject, you coward."
>
> Dashiell Hammett, *The Thin Man*

[President Putin is] absolutely having a great time. Russia is like, I mean, they're really hot stuff. . . . and now you have people in the Ukraine—who knows, set up or not—but it can't all be set up, I mean they're marching in favor of joining Russia.

April 12, 2014

> Let a crown be placed thereon, by which the world may know, that so far as we approve of monarchy, that in America the law is King. For as in absolute governments the King is law, so in free countries the law ought to be King; and there ought to be no other.
>
> Thomas Paine

Attorney General Jeff Sessions has taken a VERY weak position on Hillary Clinton crimes (where are E-mails & DNC server) & Intel leakers!

Tweet, July 25, 2017. For a time, Trump aimed angry, insulting tweets at Attorney General Jeff Sessions, one of his earliest and most loyal supporters.

> When you have a good friend that really cares for you and tries to stick in there with you, you treat them like nothing. Learn to be a good friend because one day you're gonna look up and say I lost a good friend. Learn how to be respectful to

> your friends, don't just start arguments with them and don't tell them the reason, always remember your friends will be there quicker than your family. Learn to remember you got great friends, don't forget that and they will always care for you no matter what. Always remember to smile and look up at what you got in life.
>
> Marilyn Monroe

I do have a relationship and I can tell you that he's very interested in what we're doing here today. He's probably very interested in what you and I are saying today, and I'm sure he's going to be seeing it in some form, but I do have a relationship with him and I think it's very interesting to see what's happened.

Talking about Putin and the Miss Universe pageant in Russia, September, 2013

> It is hard, I found, to be called traitor. Strange how hard it is, for it's an easy name to call another man.
>
> Ursula Le Guin, *The Left Hand of Darkness*

Have they found him guilty? I don't think they've found him guilty.

If he did it, fine. But I don't know that he did it. You know, people are saying they think it was him, it might have been him, it could have been him. But Maria, in all fairness to Putin—I don't know. You know, and I'm not saying this because he says, "Trump is brilliant and leading everybody"—the fact is that, you know, he hasn't been convicted of anything.

Fox Business interview with Maria Bartiromo on the murder of Russian security officer Alexander Litvinenko in 2016. This was his response to a British report that President Putin "probably approved" Litvinenko's January 26, 2016 murder.

> You must pursue this investigation of Watergate even if it leads to the president. I'm innocent. You've got to believe I'm innocent. If you don't, take my job.
>
> Richard M. Nixon

He's running his country and at least he's a leader. You know, unlike what we have in this country.

Talking about Vladimir Putin, MSNBC interview, December 18, 2015. In this quotation, Trump proclaims he prefers Vladimir Putin over Barack Obama, revealing a profound ignorance and disturbingly anti-democratic view.

> Vladimir Putin is a dictator. He's not a leader. Anybody who thinks otherwise doesn't know Russian history and they don't know Vladimir Putin.
>
> U.S. Senator Tim Kaine

I think many people would have held that meeting . . .

Most of the phony politicians who are Democrats who I watched over the last couple of days—most of those phonies that act holier-than-thou, if the same thing happened to them, they would have taken that meeting in a heartbeat.

Reuters interview, July 13, 2017

> Honest people don't hide their deeds.
>
> Emily Brontë, *Wuthering Heights*

While all agree the U. S. President has the complete power to pardon, why think of that when only crime so far is LEAKS against us.FAKE NEWS

Tweet, July 22, 2017

> "People have forgotten this truth," the fox said. "But you mustn't forget it. You become responsible forever for what you've tamed. You're responsible for your rose."
>
> Antoine de Saint-Exupéry, *The Little Prince*

Director Clapper reiterated what everybody, including the fake media already knows- there is "no evidence" of collusion w/ Russia and Trump.

Tweet, May 9, 2017

> The further you run from your sins, the more exhausted you are when they catch up to you. And they do. Certain. It will not fail.
>
> Dalton Russell, *Inside Man*, 2006

I think I get along with [Putin] fine. I think he would be absolutely fine. He would never keep somebody like Snowden in Russia. He hates Obama. He doesn't respect Obama. Obama doesn't like him either. But he has no respect for Obama. Has a hatred for Obama. And

Snowden is living the life. Look if that—if I'm president, Putin says, hey, boom, you're gone. I guarantee you this.

July 8, 2015, CNN interview with Anderson Cooper. As of the publication of this book, Edward Snowden is still in Russia.

> I'm convinced that before the year 2000 is over, the first child will have been born on the moon.
>
> Wernher von Braun

I always felt fine about Putin. I think that he's a strong leader. He's a powerful leader. . . . He's actually got a popularity within his country. They respect him as a leader.

MSNBC interview, December 18, 2015

> For the West, the demonization of Vladimir Putin is not a policy; it is an alibi for the absence of one. Putin is a serious strategist—on the premises of Russian history. Understanding U.S. values and psychology are not his strong suits. Nor has understanding Russian history and psychology been a strong point among U.S. policymakers.
>
> Henry Kissinger

Do you think Putin will be going to The Miss Universe Pageant in November in Moscow—if so, will he become my new best friend?

Tweet, June 19, 2013

> I am not a wolf in sheep's clothing, I'm a wolf in wolf's clothing.
>
> Ricky Gervais

As far as the reporters are concerned—as far as the reporters are concerned, obviously I don't want that to happen. I think it's terrible—horrible. But, in all fairness to Putin, you're saying he killed people. I haven't seen that. I don't know that he has. Have you been able to prove that? Do you know the names of the reporters that he's killed? Because I've been—you know, you've been hearing this, but I haven't seen the name. Now, I think it would be despicable if that took place, but I haven't seen any evidence that he killed anybody in terms of reporters.

Defending Vladimir Putin against reports that he's ordered journalists killed in Russia, ABC's This Week, *December 20, 2015.*

There are two ways to be fooled. One is to believe what isn't true; the other is to refuse to believe what is true.

Søren Kierkegaard

[Putin] called me a genius, I like him so far, I have to tell you.

Republican primary debate in South Carolina, February 13, 2016. (Putin did not, in fact, call Trump a genius. Putin said, "He's a very colorful person. Talented, without any doubt, but it's not our affair to determine our worthiness—that's up to the United States' voters. But he is absolutely the leader in the presidential race.")

The difference between appreciation and flattery? That is simple. One is sincere and the other insincere. One comes from the heart out; the other from the teeth out. One is unselfish; the other selfish. One is universally admired; the other universally condemned.

Dale Carnegie, *How to Win Friends and Influence People*

I have no relationship with him other than he called me a genius. He said, "Donald Trump is a genius and he is going to be the leader of the party and he's going to be the leader of the world or something."

> I beseech you, in the bowels of Christ, think it possible you may be mistaken.
>
> Oliver Cromwell

I own Miss Universe, I was in Russia, I was in Moscow recently and I spoke, indirectly and directly, with President Putin, who could not have been nicer, and we had a tremendous success.

May 27, 2014

> He had just about enough intelligence to open his mouth when he wanted to eat, but certainly no more.
>
> P.G. Wodehouse

The only frustration is that this Russia story is a hoax made up by the Democrats as an excuse for losing an election that they should have won because it's almost impossible for a Republican to win the Electoral College.

There was zero coordination. It's the dumbest thing I've ever heard. There's no coordination, this was a hoax, this was made up by the Democrats.

This is the greatest con job in history, where a party sits down the day after they got their ass kicked, and they say, "Huh, what's our excuse?"

It just continues and continues, and honestly it's a disgrace, and it's very bad for our country. And the Russians must be laughing, because this narrative is so bad for us as a country.

Reuters interview, July 12, 2017

> Falsehood flies, and truth comes limping after it, so that when men come to be undeceived, it is too late; the jest is over, and the tale hath had its effect: like a man, who hath thought of a good repartee when the discourse is changed, or the company parted; or like a physician, who hath found out an infallible medicine, after the patient is dead.
>
> Jonathan Swift

Funny how the failing @nytimes is pushing Dems narrative that Russia is working for me because Putin said "Trump is a genius." America 1st!

Tweet, July 27, 2016

> Look at that moon. Potato weather for sure.
>
> Thornton Wilder, *Our Town*

I actually think that he is somebody that can be dealt with. I think his dislike of President Obama is so intense, that it really has affected the whole relationship. We've driven them into the arms of China, so that now these two are together, which is also a been the great sin. Don't ever let Russia and China get together. We've driven them together. I think he is somebody that I would have a very decent relationship with if I ever win.

Interview on Fox Business, August 20, 2015

> "Name the different kinds of people," said Miss Lupescu. "Now."
>
> Bod thought for a moment. "The living," he said. "Er. The dead." He stopped. Then, ". . . Cats?" he offered, uncertainly.
>
> Neil Gaiman, *The Graveyard Book*

Look at Putin—what he's doing with Russia—I mean, you know, what's going on over there. I mean this guy has done—whether you like him or don't like him—he's doing a great job in rebuilding the image of Russia and also rebuilding Russia period.

Larry King interview, October 15, 2007

> An appeaser is one who feeds a crocodile, hoping it will eat him last.
>
> Winston S. Churchill

Most politicians would have gone to a meeting like the one Don jr attended in order to get info on an opponent. That's politics!

Tweet, July 17, 2017 about Donald Trump Jr. attending a meeting with Russians on June 9, 2016 to obtain opposition research against Hillary Clinton

> It's discouraging to think how many people are shocked by honesty and how few by deceit.
>
> Noël Coward, *Blithe Spirit*

You think of the term as being fine, but all of sudden you say, what if you're in Germany or Japan or any one of 100 different countries? You're not going to like that term. It's very insulting and Putin really put it to him [Obama] about that.

Trump agreeing with Putin about his dislike for the expression, "American exceptionalism," September 13, 2013

> You have enemies? Why, it is the story of every man who has done a great deed or created a new idea. It is the cloud which thunders around everything that shines. Fame must have enemies, as light must have gnats. Do not bother yourself about it; disdain. Keep your mind serene as you keep your life clear.
>
> Victor Hugo

I was very tough with President Putin. We have a very important relationship. It's going to be a relationship where lots of lives could be saved, like as an example with the ceasefire, which nobody else could have gotten but me."

I campaigned on strong military, strong borders, and low oil prices.

Look what I've done—oil prices have been driven down. We're sending LNG to Poland, massive shipments to Poland. That's not what Putin wants. And for the military, we've got $56 billion more of equipment than anybody ever thought of, in the last budget. Putin doesn't want that—so why would Putin want me?

It's really the one question I wish I would have asked Putin: Were you actually supporting me?

I'm very big on energy, and that's not good for Russia, because Russia makes its money with energy. That drives the price of energy down. I also am very strong on the military, very, very strong on the military. I'm also very strong on cyber.

Reuters interview, July 13, 2017

> If you once forfeit the confidence of your fellow citizens, you can never regain their respect and esteem. It is true that you may fool all of the people some of the time; you can even fool some of the people all of the time; but you can't fool all of the people all of the time.
>
> Abraham Lincoln, September 8, 1854

I've always had a good instinct about Putin. I just feel that that's a guy—and I can analyze people and you're not always right, and it could be that I won't like him. But I've always had a good feeling about him from the standpoint.

Talking with radio host Simon Conway, December 21, 2015

> Words have no power to impress the mind without the exquisite horror of their reality.
>
> Edgar Allan Poe

The meal was going toward dessert. I went down just to say hello to Melania, and while I was there I said hello to Putin. Really, pleasantries more than anything else. It was not a long conversation, but it was, you know, could be 15 minutes. Just talked about things. Actually, it was very interesting, we talked about adoption. . . .

I actually talked about Russian adoption with him. Which is interesting because it was a part of the conversation that Don had in that meeting.

Talking about his undisclosed meeting with Vladimir Putin at the G20 summit, The New York Times *interview, July 19, 2017. Adoption is a code word for discussing the Magnitsky Act and sanctions against Russia. Talking about adoptions with Vladimir Putin is anything but benign.*

> An age is called Dark, not because the light fails to shine, but because people refuse to see it.
>
> James A. Michener

I got to know [Putin] very well because we were both on "60 Minutes." We were stablemates, and we did very well that night. But, you know that.

Republican debate, November 10, 2015

> I never met Putin, I don't know who Putin is. He said one nice thing about me. He said I'm a genius. I said, "Thank you very much" to the newspaper, and that was the end of it. I never met Putin.
>
> Trump at a Florida press conference, July, 2016

There are a lot of things we could be doing economically to Russia. Russia is not strong economically and we could do a lot of different things to really do numbers on them if we wanted to.

Fox and Friends, *March 3, 2014*

> In human character, simplicity doesn't exist except among simpletons.
>
> Tennessee Williams, Where I Live: Selected Essays

Trump's Losers

Trump reminds everyone of that most hated kid in eighth grade whose language is half English, half insults. He's called people, companies, and institutions a variety of—unimaginative—insults. These insults include:

No profit company (Amazon)

Weak (Republican National Committee)

Very cowardly (James Comey)

Fools (Republican US Senators)

Incapable of understanding foreign policy (Ben Carson, a rival for the presidency, whom Trump later appointed Secretary of Health and Human Services)

Lyin' (Ted Cruz)

A pathetic figure (Jeb Bush)

Dopey (Mark Cuban)

Dumb as a rock (Don Lemon of CNN)

Irrelevant dope! (Tony Schwartz, who ghost-wrote Trump's bestselling book, *The Art of the Deal)*

Kooky (Cokie Roberts of NPR)

No focus, poor level of concentration (Ruth Marcus of the *Washington Post*)

Rapidly fading (*Morning Joe*, NBC)

Ineffective (Paul Ryan)

Goofball atheist (Penn Jillette, a magician and performer)

Crooked (Hillary Clinton)

Should be forced to take an IQ test (Rick Perry, a Trump rival for the GOP nomination for President, whom Trump appointed Secretary of Energy)

Low I.Q. Crazy Mika (Mika Brzezinski of NBC)

The list is far longer than this, but you get the idea.

As president, Trump hasn't let up with his insults. If he disagrees with you, or if you even touch his ego with a feather, he'll fire salvos of insults at you, like a child blowing spitballs. Insulting people seems to satisfy Trump; it may even relieve pent-up anxiety.

The White House defends Donald Trump as he picks apart his enemies one insult at a time. His press secretary, Sarah Huckabee Sanders, said, "I think the president is pushing back against people who attack him day after day after day. Where's the outrage on that?"

In addition to his juvenile approach to insults, Trump flings vindictiveness. He doesn't think of somebody who opposes him as disagreeing with him on just that issue, which is the way most politicians are able to get along. Senators and congressmen on opposite sides of the political aisle know they disagree on many issues, but that doesn't stop them from being friends and cooperating on other issues. Trump, in contrast, wishes his enemies the worst. He said, when talking about Rosie O'Donnell, "I like to see bad people fail." Isn't Trump sweet?

Meryl Streep, one of the most over-rated actresses in Hollywood, doesn't know me but attacked last night at the Golden Globes. She is a Hillary flunky who lost big. For the 100th time, I never "mocked" a disabled reporter (would never do that) but simply showed him "groveling" when he totally changed a 16 year old story that he had written in order to make me look bad. Just more very dishonest media!

Trump in a three-tweet-long storm on January 9, 2017, responding to Meryl Streep's speech in which she denounced Trump's mocking of a disabled New York Times *reporter. You can watch Trump here: https://www.youtube.com/watch?v=PX9reO3QnUA.*

Meryl Streep is excellent; she's a fine person, too.

Trump in a *Hollywood Reporter* interview, August 2015

Well, Rosie O'Donnell's disgusting, both inside and out. You take a look at her, she's a slob, she talks like a truck driver. . . . Rosie attacked me personally because I was very happy when her talk show failed. . . . Another thing that failed, and this was a real monster, everybody was suing her, was her magazine. her magazine called *Rosie* was a total disaster. So I love it, I gloat over it, I think it's wonderful, because I like to see bad people fail. . . .

Well, if I were running *The View*, I'd fire Rosie. I'd look her right in that fat, ugly face of hers and I'd say

"Rosie, you're fired. . . . We're all a little chubby, but Rosie's just worse than most of us. But it's not just the chubbiness. Rosie is a very unattractive person, both inside and out. . . . Rosie's a person that's very lucky to have her girlfriend, and she better be careful or I'll send one of my friends over to pick up her girlfriend, why would she stay with Rosie if she had another choice?

Interview with Megyn Kelly on Fox, 2006

> When I'm on tour, I'm in really good shape. When I get home, I cook, I eat, I get fat and happy.
>
> Pink

She gets out and she starts asking me all sorts of ridiculous questions. You could see there was blood coming out of her eyes, blood coming out of her wherever.

Talking about Megyn Kelly on August 8, 2015, after her questions to him at a presidential debate.

> Women complain about premenstrual syndrome, but I think of it as the only time of the month that I can be myself.
>
> Roseanne Barr

Cher is somewhat of a loser. She's lonely. She's unhappy. She's very miserable. And her sound-enhanced and computer-enhanced music doesn't do it for me.

May 2012 interview with Greta Van Susteren on Fox News

> "Let them speak as lewdly as they list of me . . . As long as they do not hit me, what am I the worse?"
>
> Thomas More

Barney Frank looked disgusting—nipples protruding—in his blue shirt before Congress. Very very disrespectful.

Tweet, December 22, 2011

> Adolescents are still children in that they can't yet tell the difference between make believe and fiction.
>
> Heather O'Neill

He's not a war hero. He was a war hero because he was captured. I like people who weren't captured.

Talking about Senator John McCain, who spent five years in a North Vietnamese prison, at a Family Leadership Summit in Ames, Iowa, July 2015.

For the next three or four days, I lapsed from conscious to unconsciousness. During this time, I was taken out to interrogation—which we called a "quiz"—several times. That's when I was hit with all sorts of war-criminal charges. This started on the first day. I refused to give them anything except my name, rank, serial number and date of birth. They beat me around a little bit. I was in such bad shape that when they hit me it would knock me unconscious. They kept saying, "You will not receive any medical treatment until you talk."...

I remained in solitary confinement from that time on for more than two years. I was not allowed to see or talk to or communicate with any of my fellow prisoners. My room was fairly decent-sized—I'd say it was about 10 by 10. The door was solid. There were no windows. The only ventilation came from two small holes at the top in the ceiling, about 6 inches by 4 inches. The roof was tin and it got hot as hell in there. The room was kind of dim—night and day—but they always kept on a small light bulb, so they could observe me. I was in that place for two years....

As far as this business of solitary confinement goes—the most important thing for survival is communication with someone, even if it's only a wave or a wink, a tap on the wall, or to have a guy put his thumb up. It makes all the difference.

It's vital to keep your mind occupied, and we all worked on that. Some guys were interested in mathematics, so they worked out complex formulas in their heads—we were never allowed to have writing materials. Others would build a whole house, from basement on up. I have more of a philosophical bent. I had read a lot of history. I spent days on end going back over those history books in my mind, figuring out where this country or that country went wrong, what the U.S. should do in the area of foreign affairs. I thought a lot about the meaning of life.

It was easy to lapse into fantasies. I used to write books and plays in my mind, but I doubt that any of them would have been above the level of the cheapest dime novel.

People have asked me how we could remember detailed things like the tap code, numbers, names, all sorts of things. The fact is, when you don't have anything else to think about, no outside distractions, it's easy. Since I've been back, it's very hard for me to remember simple things, like the name of someone I've just met.

During one period while I was in solitary, I memorized the names of all 335 of the men who were then prisoners of war in North Vietnam. I can still remember them.

Senator John McCain, describing his imprisonment in North Vietnam, *U.S. News and World Report*, January 28, 2008

While @BetteMidler is an extremely unattractive woman, I refuse to say that because I always insist on being politically correct.

Tweet, October 28, 2012

> If we get our self-esteem from superficial places, from our popularity, appearance, business success, financial situation, health, any of these, we will be disappointed, because no one can guarantee that we'll have them tomorrow.
>
> Kathy Ireland

Governor Pataki, who, by the way, was a failed governor in New York, a very seriously failed—he wouldn't be elected dog catcher right now.

Republican debate, September 16, 2015

> The presidency is now a cross between a popularity contest and a high school debate, with an encyclopedia of clichés.
>
> Saul Bellow

Go back to Univision.

Trump's response to journalist Jorge Ramos, who asked the candidate about his proposal to deport eleven million immigrants.

In this country American means white. Everybody else has to hyphenate.

Toni Morrison

@ariannahuff is unattractive both inside and out. I fully understand why her former husband left her for a man. He made a good decision.

Tweet, August 28, 2012

Does the mainstream media have a liberal bias? On a couple of things, maybe. Compared to the American public at large, probably a slightly higher percentage of journalists, because of their enhanced power of discernment, realize they know a gay person or two, and are, therefore, less frightened of them.

Al Franken

Did Crooked Hillary help disgusting (check out sex tape and past) Alicia M become a U.S. citizen so she could use her in the debate?

Tweet, September 30, 2016 about former Miss Universe Alicia Machado. Trump had previously said that Alicia Machado's weight gain hurt the Miss Universe pageant, which he owned.

> Insults are the arguments employed by those who are in the wrong.
>
> Jean-Jacques Rousseau

Look at that face! Would anyone vote for that? Can you imagine that, the face of our next president?!

Talking about his GOP rival Carly Fiorina, Rolling Stone *interview, September 9, 2015*

> Happiness and confidence are the prettiest things you can wear.
>
> Taylor Swift

Truly weird Senator Rand Paul of Kentucky reminds me of a spoiled brat without a properly functioning brain. He was terrible at DEBATE!

Tweet, August 10, 2015

> "How do you live with yourself, Lord Arrogant?"
>
> "Very easily, Lady Difficult. I find myself quite charming."
>
> G.A. Aiken, *About a Dragon*

Well, she has a new hairdo. Did you notice that today?

Answering a question about Hillary Clinton's appeal to voters, The Mark Levin Show, *November 11, 2015*

> What was this power, this insidious threat, this invisible gun to her head that controlled her life . . . this terror of being called names?
>
> She had stayed a virgin so she wouldn't be called a tramp or a slut; had married so she wouldn't be called an old maid; faked orgasms so she wouldn't be called frigid; had children so she wouldn't be called barren; had not been a feminist because she didn't want to be called queer and a man hater; never nagged or raised her voice so she wouldn't be called a bitch. . . .

> She had done all that and yet, still, this stranger had dragged her into the gutter with the names that men call women when they are angry.
>
> Fannie Flagg, *Fried Green Tomatoes at the Whistle Stop Cafe*

I never attacked him on his looks, and believe me there's plenty of subject matter right there.

Speaking about Senator Rand Paul, GOP debate, September 16, 2015

> "You ignorant little slug!" the Trunchbull bellowed. "You witless weed! You empty-headed hamster! You stupid glob of glue!"
>
> Roald Dahl, *Matilda*

I'm looking at guys like Marco Rubio who has the worst voting record in the United States Senate. Young guy although he sweats more than any young person I've seen in my life. I've never seen a person sweat—I have never seen a guy down water like he downs water. They bring it in in buckets for this guy.

Morning Joe, *NBC, September 24, 2015*

> Gentlemen, you can't fight in here! This is the war room!
>
> *Dr. Strangelove or: How I Learned to Stop Worrying and Love the Bomb*, 1964

I supported [John McCain], I supported him for president. I raised a million dollars for him. That's a lot of money. I supported him. He lost, he let us down. But you know, he lost. So I've never liked him much after that because I don't like losers.

Family Leadership Summit, Ames, Iowa, July 18, 2015

> A lot of comic actors derive their main force from childish behavior. Most great comics are doing such silly things; you'd say, "That's what a child would do."
>
> Gene Wilder

It's in the book that he's got a pathological temper. That's a big problem because you don't cure that. . . . As an example: child molesting. You don't cure these people. You don't cure a child molester. There's no cure for it. Pathological, there's no cure for that.

Talking about his Republican primary opponent, Ben Carson, during a CNN interview, November 12, 2015. Trump later appointed Carson Secretary of Housing and Urban Development.

> Too often character assassination has replaced debate in principle here in Washington. Destroy someone's reputation, and you don't have to talk about what he stands for.
>
> Ronald Reagan

I had a great meeting with President Obama. I never met him before. I really liked him a lot. The meeting was supposed to be 10 minutes, 15 minutes max, because there were a lot of people waiting outside, for both of us. And it ended up being—you were there—I guess an hour-and-a-half meeting, close. And it was a great chemistry. I think if he said overwhelmed, I don't think he meant that in a bad way. I think he meant that it is a very overwhelming job. But I'm not overwhelmed by it. You can do things and fix it, I think he meant it that way. He said very nice things after the meeting and I said very nice things about him. I really enjoyed my meeting with him. We have—you know, we come from different sides of the equation, but it's nevertheless something that—I didn't know if I'd like him. I probably thought that maybe I wouldn't, but I did, I did like him. I really enjoyed him a lot. I've spoken to him since the meeting.

The New York Times *interview, November 23, 2016*

How low has President Obama gone to tapp my phones during the very sacred election process. This is Nixon/Watergate. Bad (or sick) guy!

Donald Trump tweet, March 4, 2017

I refuse to call Megyn Kelly a bimbo, because that would not be politically correct. Instead I will only call her a lightweight reporter!

Twitter, January 27, 2016

Feminism is not dead, by no means. It has evolved. If you don't like the term, change it, for Goddess' sake. Call it Aphrodite, or Venus, or bimbo, or whatever you want; the name doesn't matter, as long as we understand what it is about, and we support it.

Isabel Allende

The World

The man at the helm of the world is profoundly ignorant of history and foreign affairs. He falsely claims in his book, *The Art of the Deal*, "I've read hundreds of books about China over the decades. I know the Chinese. I've made a lot of money with the Chinese. I understand the Chinese mind." But after meeting with Chinese president Xi Jinping in April 2017, Trump admitted receiving a lesson about North Korea, history, and politics from the head of a rival power: "After listening for 10 minutes, I realized it's not so easy. I felt pretty strongly that they had a tremendous power over North Korea. But it's not what you would think." Months later, Trump was back to ranting about China and North Korea on Twitter: "I am very disappointed in China. Our foolish past leaders have allowed them to make hundreds of billions of dollars a year in trade, yet they do NOTHING for us with North

Korea, just talk. We will no longer allow this to continue. China could easily solve this problem!"

Trump rants his foreign policy with what appears to be little or no consultation with foreign policy advisors.

It's dangerous and scary for a president of the United States to conduct foreign policy by tweets. It's even more dangerous for him to direct his tweets toward rivals and enemies with nuclear weapons. Maybe it would be a little less dangerous if Trump understood a thing or two about international relations and nations, but he stews in incapacity and incoherence.

Donald Trump's first international act as president was a disaster. On Saturday, January 31, ten days after his inauguration, Trump talked on the phone with Australia's prime minister, Malcolm Turnbull. Australia is one of America's closest allies. During that conversation, Trump berated Turnbull, who wanted to confirm that the United States would follow through with its agreement to admit 1,250 refugees currently being held in an Australian detention center. Trump threw a temper tantrum over the phone, telling Turnbull this was the fourth call he'd made to a head of state today and "this was the worst call by far." Trump ended the call, scheduled for an hour, after twenty-five minutes.

It's been downhill with world leaders since then. Trump turned a warm, productive, mutually beneficial relationship between the United States and Germany into that of estranged siblings. It certainly didn't help that he said German Chancellor Angela Merkel was "ruining Germany" by letting in immigrants.

Perhaps the most pressing international issue for America is North Korea. (Until the Middle East erupts again. Or until global warming manifests some catastrophe, like famine, the spread of disease, or a city submerged. Or until . . .) At his second full Cabinet meeting, when asked about North Korea, Trump asserted, "We will handle North Korea. We are gonna be able to handle them. It will be handled. We handle everything." That's it. That's Trump's grand plan for North Korea, a tepid assurance that is not reassuring at all.

If America wants to guide the future, and if America wants the world to become a better place—more democratic, peaceful, and prosperous—it has to lead. Trump doesn't lead. He staggers.

At a certain point, when that sucker comes by you, you gotta shoot. You gotta shoot. I mean, you gotta shoot.

Trump talking about Russian jets doing barrel rolls over U.S. Air Force jets, May 2, 2016

> The fury of a demon instantly possessed me. I knew myself no longer. My original soul seemed, at once, to take its flight from my body; and a more than fiendish malevolence, gin-nurtured, thrilled every fibre of my frame.
>
> Edgar Allan Poe, "The Black Cat"

North Korea best not make any more threats to the United States. They will be met with fire and fury like the world has never seen.

Bridgewater, New Jersey, August 8, 2017. John Mecklin, editor-in-chief of the Bulletin of the Atomic Scientists, *said about Trump's statement, "That is about the stupidest and most dangerous statement I have ever heard an American president make."*

> It's a near miracle that nuclear war has so far been avoided.
>
> Noam Chomsky

When the students poured into Tiananmen Square, the Chinese government almost blew it. Then they were vicious, they were horrible, but they put it down with strength. That shows you the power of strength. Our country is right now perceived as weak, . . . as being spit on by the rest of the world.

Playboy *magazine interview, March 1, 1990. An estimated 10,000 people were arrested and hundreds or thousands of people were killed by the Chinese government during the Tiananmen Square protests in 1989. Several dozen participants were later executed. Trump supports that.*

> It is hard, I submit, to loathe bloodshed, including war, more than I do, but it is still harder to exceed my loathing of the very nature of totalitarian states in which massacre is only an administrative detail.
>
> Vladimir Nabokov

I am very disappointed in China. Our foolish past leaders have allowed them to make hundreds of billions of dollars a year in trade, yet they do NOTHING for us with North Korea, just talk. We will no longer allow this to continue. China could easily solve this problem!

July 29, 2017

Great minds have purposes; others have wishes.

Washington Irving

Finland is respected by Russia. Finland has been free of Russia, really—just about one of the few countries in the region that has been—for 100 years.

August 28, 2017. Russia invaded Finland in 1939.

A man is responsible for his ignorance.

Milan Kundera, *Laughable Loves*

So I deal with foreign countries, and despite what you may read I have unbelievable relationships with all of the foreign leaders. They like me. I like them. You know, it's amazing. So I'll call, like, major—major countries, and I'll be dealing with the prime minister or the president. And I'll say, how are you doing? Oh, don't know, don't know, not well, Mr. President, not well. I said, well, what's the problem? Oh, GDP 9 percent, not well. And I'm saying to myself, here we are at like 1 percent, dying, and they're at 9 percent and they're unhappy. So, you know, and these are like countries, you know, fairly large, like 300 million people. You know, a lot of people say—they say, well, but the United States is large. And then you call places like

Malaysia, Indonesia, and you say, you know, how many people do you have? And it's pretty amazing how many people they have. So China's going to be at 7 or 8 percent, and they have a billion-five, right? So we should do really well.

The Wall Street Journal *interview, July 25, 2017, talking like a nine-year-old after receiving an atlas as a present. Except nine-year-olds are able to hold a thought in their heads through to completion.*

> Following the light of the sun, we left the Old World.
>
> Christopher Columbus

The World as we know it is falling apart. Much of the blame can be attributed to the fact that the United States is no longer respected!

Tweet, August 9, 2014

> I will tell only of the lone tomb in the darkest of the hillside thickets; the deserted tomb of the Hydes, an old and exalted family whose last direct descendant had been laid within its black recesses many decades before my birth.
>
> HP Lovecraft, "The Tomb," 1917

It is always a great honor to be so nicely complimented by a man so highly respected within his own country and beyond.

After Putin called Trump a "talented person" and "the absolute leader of the presidential race," December 17, 2015

> I can live for two months on a good compliment.
>
> Mark Twain

Be prepared, there is a small chance that our horrendous leadership could unknowingly lead us into World War III.

Tweet, Aug 31, 2013

> North Korea best not make any more threats to the United States. They will be met with fire and fury like the world has never seen.
>
> President Trump, Bedminster, New Jersey, August 8, 2017

I built a truly great company worth many billions of dollars. That is a big part of the reason I was elected. As

President, I can make far better deals with foreign countries than Congress.

The concluding paragraph to Trump's signing statement for Countering America's Adversaries Through Sanctions Act, otherwise known as the Russian Sanctions Bill. It's an example of Trump's hubris, ego—and the fact that he doesn't know that international relations aren't a business deal. The signing statement makes no mention of Russian efforts to interfere with the U.S. presidential election.

> Few businessmen are capable of being in politics, they don't understand the democratic process, they have neither the tolerance or the depth it takes. Democracy isn't a business.
>
> Malcolm Forbes

If the morons who killed all of those people at Charlie Hebdo would have just waited, the magazine would have folded—no money, no success!

Tweet, January 14, 2015. Two brothers who were members of Al-Qaeda attacked the Paris-based satirical magazine, Charlie Hebdo, *killing twelve people and injuring eleven others. Trump, in this tweet, shows how little empathy he has for other human beings.*

> The opposite of love is not hate, it's indifference. The opposite of art is not ugliness, it's indifference. The opposite of faith is not heresy, it's indifference. And the opposite of life is not death, it's indifference.
>
> Elie Wiesel

When Mexico sends its people, they're not sending the best. They're sending people that have lots of problems and they're bringing those problems. They're bringing drugs, they're bringing crime. They're rapists and some, I assume, are good people, but I speak to border guards and they're telling us what we're getting.

June 16, 2015

> Nearly all Americans have ancestors who braved the oceans—liberty-loving risk takers in search of an ideal—the largest voluntary migrations in recorded history. Immigration is not just a link to America's past; it's also a bridge to America's future.
>
> George W. Bush

Mexican leaders and negotiators are much tougher and smarter than those of the U.S. Mexico is killing us on jobs and trade. WAKE UP!

Tweet, July 3 2015

> I like surfing in Mexico a whole lot better than sitting with people in Washington that I don't even like.
>
> Jesse Ventura

Hopefully we will never have to use this power, but there will never be a time that we are not the most powerful nation in the world!

Tweet, August 9, 2017

> Put that needed code number in a little capsule, and then implant that capsule right next to the heart of a volunteer. The volunteer would carry with him a big, heavy butcher knife as he accompanied the President. If the President wanted to fire nuclear weapons, the only way he could do so would be for him first, with his own hands, to kill one human being.
>
> The President says, "George, I'm sorry, but tens of millions must die." He has to look at somebody

and realize what death is—what an innocent death is. Blood on the White House carpet.

Roger Fisher, *The Bulletin of the Atomic Scientists,* March 1981

He's running his country and at least he's a leader, unlike what we have in this country. I think our country does plenty of killing also.

MSNBC, Morning Joe, *Dec. 18, 2015, Trump talking about allegations Russia's President Putin ordered the killings of journalists. In this single statement, Trump equates America with Putin's repression.*

When you are young, you are a little naive.

Maria Sharapova

Just arrived in Scotland. People are going wild over the vote. They took their country back. Just like we'll take our country back. No games.

Tweet after the Brexit vote. Scotland, however, voted 68 percent to 32 percent to remain in the European Union.

> @realDonaldTrump You utter and complete eejit. Landslide vote to Remain from Scotland, UK vote only just managed to force us to leave.
>
> Lean MacKinnon, one of countless Scotlanders who responded to Trump's misinformed tweet.

America is proud to stand shoulder-to-shoulder w/a free & ind UK. We stand together as friends, as allies, & as a people w/a shared history.

Tweet, Jun 24 2016

> He remembered his uncle saying once how little vocabulary man really needed to get comfortably and even efficiently through his life, how not only in the individual but within his whole type and race and kind a few simple cliches served his few simple passions and needs and lusts.
>
> William Faulkner, Intruder in the Dust

North Korea just stated that it is in the final stages of developing a nuclear weapon capable of reaching parts of the U.S. It won't happen!

Tweet, January 3, 2017

"U.S. Confirms North Korea Fired Intercontinental Ballistic Missile"

New York Times, July 4, 2017

"North Korean ICBM test: Alaska, Hawaii pols demand better missile defense"

Fox News, July 5, 2017

I think he's a threat to this country. I mean he must have some kind of thing going because you know, when you see that he won't even call them by their name—it's radical Islamic terrorism and he won't even acknowledge it—it's like they're coming out of Denmark of something.

Talking about President Barack Obama, WRKO radio, Boston, Massachusetts, November 18, 2015

I do this real moron thing, and it's called thinking. And apparently I'm not a very good American because I like to form my own opinions.

George Carlin

The #IranDeal is a catastrophe that must be stopped. Will lead to at least partial world destruction & will make Iran a force like never before.

Tweet, August 11, 2015

> President Trump agreed on Monday to certify again that Iran is complying with an international nuclear agreement that he has strongly criticized.
>
> *The New York Times*, July 17, 2017

He then went into the history of China and Korea. Not North Korea, Korea. And you know, you're talking about thousands of years . . . and many wars. And Korea actually used to be a part of China. And after listening for 10 minutes, I realized that it's not so easy.

The Wall Street Journal *interview, April 12, 2017, in which Trump admitted not understanding China's relationship to North Korea, and why China can't control North Korea, until China's president explained it to him. Think about that: The President of the United States is being schooled in foreign policy, not by his advisors, but by China's president.*

> We are all born ignorant, but one must work hard to remain stupid.
>
> Benjamin Franklin

Donald J. Trump is calling for a complete and total shutdown of Muslims entering the United States until our country's representatives can figure out what the hell is going on.

At a campaign rally in Charleston, South Carolina, December 2015

> Comments that suggest that Muslims should be banned from the United States are offensive and unconstitutional.
>
> Vice President Mike Pence

North Korea has just launched another missile. Does this guy have anything better to do with his life? Hard to believe that South Korea and Japan will put up with this much longer. Perhaps China will put a heavy move on North Korea and end this nonsense once and for all!

A two-tweetstorm, July 3, 2017

> A nuclear program has arguably worked as a deterrent for North Korea and other states. Would Muammar Gaddafi have been deposed and summarily killed if Libya had had nuclear weapons? Iranians might not think so.
>
> Richard Engel

He's a fantastic guy. . . . He took control of Egypt. And he really took control of it.

Talking about Egyptian President, Abdel Fattah el-Sisi, interview with Lou Dobbs of Fox Business, September 22, 2016.

> If this were a dictatorship it would be a heck of a lot easier. . . . As long as I'm the dictator. Hehehe.
>
> George W. Bush

You know what uranium is, right? It's a thing called nuclear weapons and other things. Like lots of things are done with uranium, including some bad things.

February 16, 2017

> "At the moment that we hear the shriek of the melting telephone in Moscow, I will order a SAC squadron which is at this moment flying over New York City to drop four 20-megaton bombs on that city in precisely the pattern and altitude in which our planes have been ordered to bomb Moscow. They will use the Empire State Building for ground zero. When we hear the second shriek over the conference line we will know that your delegate to the United Nations is gone and along with him, New York."

"Holy Mother of God," Khrushchev said. His voice seemed almost like a pant.

Then there was a deep silence. Suddenly, like a mechanical mockery, there was a flare-up of static on the line. It sounded like some macabre laugh, something torn from the soul of the mechanical system. "There is no other way, Mr. Premier, that I could think to demonstrate to you our sincerity," the President said softly.

Failsafe, by Eugene Burdick and Harvey Wheeler, from the passage in which the president offers to sacrifice New York City to prevent a thermonuclear war because the U.S. accidentally destroyed Moscow.

[ISIS has] better access to internet than we do. I mean, they're recruiting people from our country and who knows what they're planning.

ABC interview with George Stephanopoulos, November 8, 2015

Crying wolf is a real danger.

David Attenborough

Larry, the country is losing two hundred billion dollars a year. Two hundred billion. This country cannot continue to lose two hundred billion dollars. Japan is one of the wealthiest machines ever created. Saudi Arabia—and it's not—hey, lemme tell ya, I'm a big beneficiary of Japan. They buy my apartments in spades. They're fine people. But they must be—they're laughing to themselves as to what's happening over here. We're not kidding ourselves. They're laughing to themselves, Larry, as to what's happening with this country.

I watch—and again, it's a very important point. Japan is a money machine. Saudi Arabia is a money machine. Kuwait. These are money machines, the greatest ever created. The United States is—if it were a corporation, it would be bankrupt. It's losing two hundred billion dollars a year. For years now it's been losing that. What right do we have to go out and defend—why aren't these countries, these wealthy money machines, paying us for the defense of their freedom and their nations? Why aren't they paying us?

I don't believe we should be. I think Japan should certainly make a contribution. Japan is—one of the reasons they're so successful is they don't have to worry about defense, because why should they worry about defense when the United States will do it for nothing? I mean, it's crazy. Saudi Arabia. I mean, you saw what happened with Saudi Arabia. We're going through the Gulf. We have old-fashioned, obsolete minesweepers. We ask Saudi Arabia for the use of their minesweepers, which are the best made, the most modern, the best, and they say no? Who are they to tell us no? We're not going to give you our minesweepers? It's ridiculous. They're only there, they're only there because of us as far as that's concerned. We are protective of Saudi Arabia. They should pay for that.

Larry King Live, *September 2, 1987*

> Security assistance programs, an essential complement to our defense effort, directly enhance the security of the United States. Development assistance also contributes to this effort by supplementing the indigenous efforts of recipients to achieve economic growth and meet the basic needs of their peoples. Progress in both of these areas will contribute to regional stability and to a more peaceful world, both of which are central U.S. policy objectives.
>
> Ronald Reagan, December 29, 1981

We look forward to a lot of very positive happenings for Russia, and for the United States, and for everybody concerned. And it's an honor to be with you.

At a meeting with Russian President Vladimir Putin, July 7, 2017

> Our nation marches closer to Trumpism each day, a path paved with reckless Tweets and the normalization of the ugly and the absurd.
>
> David Brock

He is the founder of ISIS. He's the founder of ISIS, okay? He's the founder. He founded ISIS and I would say the co-founder would be crooked Hillary Clinton.

Talking about President Obama, campaign rally, Florida, August 10, 2016

> Rumor:
> Upon my tongues continual slanders ride,
> The which in every language I pronounce,
> Stuffing the ears of men with false reports.
>
> William Shakespeare, *Henry IV, Part 2*

My experience yesterday in Poland was a great one. Thank you to everyone, including the haters, for the great reviews of the speech!

Tweet, July 7, 2017. It's as if Trump only hears the good news about his public performances. Wait! That's exactly what happens. Vice News reported on August 8, 2017, "Trump gets a folder full of positive news about himself twice a day. "Maybe it's good for the country that the president is in a good mood in the morning," one former RNC official said."

> The smaller the mind, the greater the conceit.
>
> Aesop

Well, I can tell you, some of the people I'm running against don't have a clue as to—we're talking now Republicans—as to what to do about what we are talking about, devaluations. And I do. That's what I do, and I am really good at this stuff. I will make great deals with China and they will like us more than they do now. You know they don't even like us. You know in *Businessweek* magazine, they did a story a while ago about one of the ten things that the Chinese most want. One of the ten things was "Anything Trump." And I thought about that. And they respect me. They have to respect you. China does not respect us and they don't respect our leaders. I have done great in China.

The Economist *interview, September 3, 2015*

> I want to help the helpless, but I don't want to help the clueless.
>
> Dennis Miller

If [Putin] says great things about me, I'm going to say great things about him. I've already said, he is really very much of a leader. I mean, you can say, "Oh, isn't that a terrible thing"—the man has very strong control over a country. Now, it's a very different system, and I don't happen to like the system. But certainly, in that system, he's been a leader, far more than our president has been a leader.

Interview with Matt Lauer, NBC, Sept. 7, 2016. In this statement, Trump praises Russia's president.

Enlightened despots are mythical creatures; real despots seem more interested in stealing money or installing their sons after them.

Elliott Abrams

I have a very good relationship with him. I think he's a tremendous guy. But don't forget. He's for China. I'm for the U.S.

Talking about China's president, Xi Jinping, July 2017

A day without sunshine is, like, you know, night.

Steve Martin

Great relationship with [German Chancellor Angela] Merkel, one of the best. In fact so good she invited my daughter over. She loves Ivanka. Ivanka was over there and did great. But no, I have a very good relationship with all of them, including Australia. You saw that the other night, right. You know they all said I hung up and I slammed the phone on him. I didn't do that. I mean, it was a little testy for a while because Obama made a ridiculous deal. But that wasn't [Australian Prime Minister] Malcolm [Turnbull]'s fault. But we have a very good relationship with Australia and him. Which I think the other night showed.

. . . I get back [former Egyptian prisoner] Aya [Hijazi]. Nobody could have done that. Nobody else could have done that. They could have negotiated—how tough is [Egyptian leader Abdel Fattah] el Sisi, right? Nobody else could have done—and he's a great guy. Nobody else could have gotten her back. She would have been in jail for twenty-eight years. And that's not twenty-eight years you're going away for one. That's twenty-eight years meaning twenty-eight years.

Time *magazine interview, May 11, 2017*

> There's a whole lot of people in trouble tonight
> From the disease of conceit
> Whole lot of people seeing double tonight
> From the disease of conceit
> Give ya delusions of grandeur
> And a evil eye
> Give you the idea that
> You're too good to die
> Then they bury you from your head to your feet
> From the disease of conceit
>
> Bob Dylan, "Disease of Conceit"

We have to humiliate the enemy. And if we don't humiliate them, we're going to have our kids continuing to go and fight for ISIS. We have kids leaving this country because they're so damned good at the internet, ISIS, they're better at the internet than Google. You know it's a smart enemy. Believe it or not. And these kids are going over and fighting.

Time *magazine interview, May 11, 2017*

> He's going to be president of the Queen's County Bullies Association.
>
> *Anthony Scaramucci, President Trump's communications director for one week, talking about then-candidate Donald Trump in August 2015.*

France is America's first and oldest ally. A lot of people don't know that. . . . France helped us secure our independence, a lot of people forget.

Paris, France, July 13, 2017

> "Anyone with half a mind could see that," said Tiffany.
>
> Miss Tick sighed. "Yes. But sometimes it's so hard to find half a mind when you need one."
>
> Terry Pratchett, *Wee Free Men*

Well, I don't like it, it's very far away. I do not like it. It's very hostile. It's a hostile move. And I would be talking to them very seriously about it. However, it is very far away, and we have a lot of problems, okay?

The Economist *interview in response to the question, "What would President Trump do about China building reefs and air bases in the South China Sea?" September 3, 2015.*

> I should not proceed by land to the East, as is customary, but by a Westerly route, in which direction we have hitherto no certain evidence that any one has gone.
>
> Christopher Columbus

You take the oil. It's simple. You take the oil. There are certain areas which ISIS has the oil and you take the oil, you keep it. You just go in and take it.

The Economist *interview in response to the question, "How do you keep that oil [from the Middle East]?," September 3, 2015*

And a follow-up question from The Economist*: "And would you have American troops guarding that?"*

Yes, we could do that very easily. . . . I would have American forces guarding the oil, absolutely. Nobody is going to take it back. Without our very strong approval. Nobody else is taking it back.

> ISIS wouldn't have existed without the US invasion of Iraq. It was born out of the Sunnis' feeling

> of alienation, their belief that they'd been pushed aside—which, of course, they had been. Sunnis suffered a thirteen-century-old injustice with power stripped from them by Washington and given to Iraqi Shiites and their coreligionists in Iran. This grievance is at the core of ISIS ideology. Simply put, no Iraq war, no ISIS.
>
> Richard Engel, *And Then All Hell Broke Loose: Two Decades in the Middle East*

I will build a great wall—and nobody builds walls better than me, believe me—and I'll build them very inexpensively. I will build a great, great wall on our southern border, and I will make Mexico pay for that wall. Mark my words.

June 2015

> Mr. Gorbachev, tear down this wall.
>
> Ronald Reagan, June 12, 1987

I've had a lot of briefings that are very, don't want to say "scary," because I'll solve the problems. But . . . we have some big enemies out there in this country and we have some very big enemies—very big and, in some cases, strong enemies.

January 20, 2017, before being inaugurated

> If you break your neck, if you have nothing to eat, if your house is on fire, then you got a problem. Everything else is inconvenience.
>
> Robert Fulghum

Trade between China and North Korea grew almost 40% in the first quarter. So much for China working with us—but we had to give it a try!

Tweet, July 5, 2017

> We know little of the things for which we pray.
>
> Geoffrey Chaucer, *The Canterbury Tales*

A big thing we have with China was, if they could help us with North Korea, that would be great. They have pressures that are tough pressures, and I understand. And you know, don't forget, China, over the many years, has been at war with Korea—you know, wars with Korea. It's not like, oh, gee, you just do whatever we say. They've had numerous wars with Korea.

Interview aboard Air Force One, July 12, 2017

> War is what happens when language fails.
>
> Margaret Atwood

The era of strategic patience with the North Korea regime has failed. That patience is over.

July 1, 2017

> One day the great European War will come out of some damned foolish thing in the Balkans.
>
> Otto von Bismarck, 1888

They have an 8,000 year culture. So when they see 1776—to them, that's like a modern building. The White House was started—was essentially built in 1799. To us, that's really old. To them, that's like a super modern building, right?

Interview aboard Air Force One, July 12, 2017, talking about China

> Eragon looked back at him, confused. "I don't understand."
>
> "Of course you don't," said Brom impatiently. "That's why I'm teaching you and not the other way around."
>
> Christopher Paolini, *Eragon*

You know, back when they did NATO there was no such thing as terrorism.

Associated Press Interview, April 22, 2017

> If you don't know history, then you don't know anything. You are a leaf that doesn't know it is part of a tree.
>
> Michael Crichton

We get almost nothing for what we do. We defend the world. We defend so many countries. We get nothing. They get everything. We get nothing. South Korea's going to have to start ponying up, okay? And we'll do it in a very nice manner. They'll like us even more than they like us now.

Fox & Friends *interview, January 2016*

> The thing that should most concern us is a shift in American foreign policy. We have had a bipartisan belief in American foreign policy based on the post-World War II institutions that believed in democratic global world, which Russia and the Soviet Union was often seen as hostile to. And most Republicans and Democrats have always basically believed in this world order. Donald Trump and Vladimir Putin and maybe Marine Le Pen do not agree with this basic structure of the world.
>
> David Brooks

For a religious leader to question a person's faith is disgraceful. I am proud to be a Christian. . . . If and when the Vatican is attacked by ISIS, which as everyone knows is ISIS's ultimate trophy, I can promise you that the Pope would have only wished and prayed that Donald Trump would have been President because this would not have happened.

February 8, 2016, campaign press release responding to Pope Francis' suggestion that Trump isn't a Christian because, said the Pope, "A person who thinks only about building walls, wherever they may be, and not building bridges, is not Christian."

> Being a Christian is more than just an instantaneous conversion—it is a daily process whereby you grow to be more and more like Christ.
>
> Billy Graham

They'd probably wipe them out pretty quick. If they fight, you know what, that'd be a terrible thing. . . . But if they do, they do. Good luck, enjoy yourself, folks.

Wisconsin rally, March 2016, speaking about thermonuclear war, North Korea, and whether Japan should become a nuclear armed nation.

> Every inhabitant of this planet must contemplate the day when this planet may no longer be habitable. Every man, woman and child lives under a nuclear Sword of Damocles, hanging by the slenderest of threads, capable of being cut at any moment by accident or miscalculation or by madness. The weapons of war must be abolished before they abolish us.
>
> John F. Kennedy

Mexico's court system corrupt.I want nothing to do with Mexico other than to build an impenetrable WALL and stop them from ripping off U.S.

Tweet, March 6, 2015

> I took a rant-sized breath.
>
> Scott Westerfeld, *So Yesterday*

When it came time to, as an example, send out the 59 missiles, the Tomahawks in Syria. I'm saying to myself, "You know, this is more than just like, 79 missiles. This is death that's involved."

Associated Press interview, April 22, 2017. Trump misremembered how many missiles the United States launched.

> Right now I'm having amnesia and déjà vu at the same time. I think I've forgotten this before.
>
> Steven Wright

When Iran, when they circle our beautiful destroyers with their little boats, and they make gestures at our people that they shouldn't be allowed to make, they will be shot out of the water.

Pensacola, Florida, September 9, 2016

> Where to look if you've lost your mind?
>
> Bernard Malamud, *The Fixer*

The Panama Canal is doing quite well, I think we did a good job building it.

Talking with the President Juan Carlos Varela of Panama, June 2017, as if the Panama Canal had been recently completed. President Varela replied. Trump asked, "Right?" President Varela replied, "One hundred years ago."

> Who's Britannica to tell me that the Panama Canal was built in 1914? If I want to say that it was built in 1941, that's my right as an American.
>
> Stephen Colbert

Can I be honest are you? Maybe it's going to have to be time to change, because so many people, you have Pakistan has it, you have China has it. You have so many other countries are now having it. . . . Now, wouldn't you rather, in a certain sense, have Japan have nuclear weapons when North Korea has nuclear weapons?

In a CNN interview in March, 2016, about whether Japan should have nuclear weapons. In April in a Fox interview with Chris Wallace, Trump elaborated: "It's not like, gee whiz, nobody has them. So, North Korea has nukes. Japan has a problem with that. I mean, they have a big problem with that. Maybe they would in fact be better off if they defend themselves from North Korea. . . . Including with nukes, yes, including with nukes."

The heat was tremendous. And I felt like my body was burning all over. For my burning body the cold water of the river was as precious as the treasure. Then I left the river, and I walked along the railroad tracks in the direction of my home. On the way, I ran into an another friend of mine, Tokujiro Hatta. I wondered why the soles of his feet were badly burnt. It was unthinkable to get burned there. But it was undeniable fact the soles were peeling and red muscle was exposed. Even I myself was terribly burnt, I could not go home ignoring him. I made him crawl using his arms and knees. Next, I made him stand on his heels and I supported him. We walked heading toward my home repeating the two methods. When we were resting because we were so exhausted, I found my grandfather's brother and his wife, in other words, great uncle and great aunt, coming toward us. That was quite coincidence. As you know, we have a proverb about meeting Buddha in Hell. My encounter with my relatives at that time was just like that. They seem to be the Buddha to me wandering in the living hell.

Akihiro Takahashi, a Hiroshima survivor, who was fourteen on August 6, 1945

Last week, I read 2,300 Humvees—these are big vehicles—were left behind for the enemy. 2,000? You would say maybe two, maybe four? 2,300 sophisticated vehicles, they ran, and the enemy took them.

From Trump's speech announcing his candidacy for president, June 16, 2015

> And in the absence of facts, myth rushes in, the kudzu of history.
>
> Stacy Schiff, *Cleopatra: A Life*

[Vladimir Putin] is not going into Ukraine, OK, just so you understand. He's not gonna go into Ukraine, all right? You can mark it down. You can put it down.

ABC's This Week with George Stephanopoulos, July 31, 2016. When Stephanopoulos pointed out that Russia was already in Ukraine, Trump replied, "Okay—well, he's there in a certain way. But I'm not there. You have Obama there. And frankly, that whole part of the world is a mess under Obama with all the strength that you're talking about and all of the power of NATO and all of this. In the meantime, he's going away. He takes Crimea."

> From this point forth, we shall be leaving the firm foundation of fact and journeying together

> through the murky marshes of memory into thickets of wildest guesswork.
>
> J.K. Rowling, *Harry Potter and the Half-Blood Prince*

When will the U.S. stop sending $'s to our enemies, i.e. Mexico and others.

Tweet July 11, 2014

> For the United States, supporting international development is more than just an expression of our compassion. It is a vital investment in the free, prosperous, and peaceful international order that fundamentally serves our national interest.
>
> Former U.S. Secretary of State Condoleezza Rice, October 2008 at the White House Summit on International Development

Europe is a big place, I'm not going to take cards off the table.

Answering a question about using nuclear weapons in Europe, The O'Reilly Factor, *March 31, 2016*

> I saw a bright blast, and I saw yellow and silver and orange and all sorts of colors that I can't explain. Those colors came and attacked us, and the ceiling beams of the wooden school along with the glass from the window pane all shattered and blew away all at once.
>
> [I saw] people whose eyeballs had popped out their sockets. There were those who held their babies—burnt black; they themselves had no skin. There were those whose intestines had come out of their bodies, and confused they struggled to put them back in.
>
> Hiroshima survivor Michiko Kodoma, who was seven when Hiroshima was bombed. Hibakusha, 被爆者, are the survivors the bombings of Hiroshima and Nagasaki.

China's Communist Party has now publicly praised Obama's reelection. They have never had it so good. Will own America soon.

Tweet, November 8, 2012

> You are not entitled to your opinion. You are entitled to your informed opinion. No one is entitled to be ignorant.
>
> Harlan Ellison

If we would have taken the oil, you wouldn't have ISIS.

Talking about Iraq's oil, September 7, 2016

> Never interrupt your enemy when he is making a mistake.
>
> Napoléon Bonaparte

Despite what you have heard from the FAKE NEWS, I had a GREAT meeting with German Chancellor Angela Merkel. Nevertheless, Germany owes vast sums of money to NATO & the United States must be paid more for the powerful, and very expensive, defense it provides to Germany!

A two-tweet storm, March 18, 2017

> The Parties to this Treaty reaffirm their faith in the purposes and principles of the
>
> Charter of the United Nations and their desire to live in peace with all peoples and all Governments.
>
> They are determined to safeguard the freedom, common heritage and civilisation of their peoples, founded on the principles of democracy, individual liberty and the rule of law. They seek to promote stability and well-being in the North Atlantic area.

They are resolved to unite their efforts for collective defence and for the preservation of peace and security. They therefore agree to this North Atlantic Treaty.

The North Atlantic Treaty, 1949

The Campaign and Election

There's a lot you can say about Trump and the 2016 presidential campaign. He lied a lot. He was feisty. Trump understood his base, and he understood that they didn't care what he said, how often or how deeply he falsified facts, as long as he spoke their language, a language of callousness and, for many, bigotry and xenophobia.

As a political outsider, as somebody who'd never held elected office or served in the military, Trump had a powerful tool that he was willing and able to deploy: Trump was unconstrained by the niceties of political language. He could insult—"Lyin' Ted Cruz" and "Crooked Hillary"—and repeat those phrases over and over again.

At the start of the GOP nomination process, there were seventeen candidates; John Kasich, Ted Cruz, Donald Trump, George Pataki, Marco Rubio, Bobby

Jindal, Mike Huckabee, Lindsay Graham, Ben Carson, Jeb Bush, Jim Gilmore, Chris Christie, Carly Fiorina, Scott Walker, Rick Santorum, Rand Paul, and Rick Perry. Trump positioned himself as an outsider and a rebel, unruly and not constrained by social or political norms. It was a strategy that succeeded (perhaps with a little help from the Russians).

Despite Trump's gross speech and emptiness when it came to issues, he won. How vacuous was (and still apparently may be) Trump's mind? In response to a question about the nuclear triad, Trump said, "Well, first of all, I think we need somebody absolutely that we can trust, who is totally responsible, who really knows what he or she is doing. That is so powerful and so important. And one of the things that I'm frankly most proud of is that in 2003, 2004, I was totally against going into Iraq because you're going to destabilize the Middle East. I called it. I called it very strongly. And it was very important. But we have to be extremely vigilant and extremely careful when it comes to nuclear. Nuclear changes the whole ballgame. Frankly, I would have said get out of Syria; get out—if we didn't have the power of weaponry today. The power is so massive that we can't just leave areas that 50 years ago or 75 years ago we wouldn't care. It was hand-to-hand combat. The biggest problem this world has today is not President Obama with global warming, which is inconceivable, this is what he's saying. The biggest problem we have is nuclear—nuclear proliferation and having some maniac, having some madman go out and get a nuclear weapon. That's in my opinion, that is the single biggest problem that our country faces right now." Remember, he was asked about the nuclear triad, our system of nuclear deterrence that uses land-based missiles, submarines, and aircraft.

When pressed on this question and asked which of the three legs of the nuclear triad should receive priority, Trump answered, "I think—I think, for me, nuclear is just the power, the devastation is very important to me."

Trump's joy in speaking in vulgarities and his near-complete lack of knowledge about issues worried members of his own party. But they thought he'd either simmer down or be educable, or both, if he got elected.

I'm Donald Trump. I wrote the *Art of the Deal.* I say not in a braggadocious way. I've made billions and billions of dollars dealing with people all over the world, and I want to put whatever that talent is to work for this country so we have great trade deals, we make our country rich again, we make it great again. We build our military, we take care of our vets, we get rid of Obamacare, and we have a great life together.

Opening statement at the Republican debate, September 16, 2015

> He thinks himself rather an exceptional young man, thoroughly sophisticated, well adjusted to his environment, and somewhat more significant than anyone else he knows.
>
> F. Scott Fitzgerald, *The Beautiful and Damned*

Ladies and gentleman I want to make a major announcement today. I would like to promise and pledge to all of my voters and supporters, and to all of the people of the United States, that I will totally accept the results of this great and historic presidential election—if I win.

Campaign rally, Delaware, Ohio, October 20, 2016

> Absolute power turns its possessors not into a God but an anti-God. For God turned clay into men, while the absolute despot turns men into clay.
>
> Eric Hoffer

In addition to winning the Electoral College in a landslide, I won the popular vote if you deduct the millions of people who voted illegally.

Tweet, November 28 2016

> The trust of the innocent is the liar's most useful tool.
>
> Stephen King, *Needful Things*

I don't quite get it—if I'm going to do a job with the lowering taxes, better health care, take care of people, take care of hospitalization, all the things we're doing, because there's no plan now. You would think that people would like that. And they don't. . . . I used to get the credit in business but they want to belittle everything you do. Business is easier because you put something up, it's good, whatever.

But the politics is tough.

Time *magazine interview, May 11, 2017*

One of the major problems encountered in time travel is . . . simply one of grammar, and the main work to consult in this matter is Dr. Dan Streetmentioner's Time Traveler's Handbook of 1001 Tense Formations. It will tell you, for instance, how to describe something that was about to happen to you in the past before you avoided it by time-jumping forward two days in order to avoid it. The event will be described differently according to whether you are talking about it from the standpoint of your own natural time, from a time in the further future, or a time in the further past and is further complicated by the possibility of conducting conversations while you are actually traveling from one time to another with the intention of becoming your own mother or father.

Most readers get as far as the Future Semiconditionally Modified Subinverted Plagal Past Subjunctive Intentional before giving up; and in fact in later editions of the book all pages beyond this point have been left blank to save on printing costs.

The Hitchhiker's Guide to the Galaxy skips lightly over this tangle of academic abstraction, pausing only to note that the term "Future Perfect" has been abandoned since it was discovered not to be.

Douglas Adams, *The Restaurant at the End of the Universe*

I know where she went. It's disgusting, I don't want to talk about it. No, it's too disgusting. Don't say it, it's disgusting.

Commenting on Hillary Clinton's bathroom break before their December 2015 debate

> Then came the time for the evening visit to the toilet, for which, in all likelihood, you had waited, all atremble, all day. How relieved, how eased, the whole world suddenly became! How the great questions all simplified themselves at the same instant—did you feel it?
>
> Aleksandr Solzhenitsyn, *The Gulag Archipelago*

Hillary wants to abolish, essentially abolish, the Second Amendment. By the way, and if she gets to pick her judges, nothing you can do, folks. If she gets to pick her judges—nothing you can do, folks. Although, the Second Amendment people. Maybe there is. I don't know.

Wilmington, North Carolina campaign rally, August 9, 2016. Many people interpreted this comment to hint at violence against Hillary Clinton.

> It has too often been too easy for rulers and governments to incite man to war.
>
> Lester B. Pearson

I would rarely leave the White House because there's so much work to be done. I would not be a president who took vacations. I would not be a president that takes time off.

June 2015

> Lying is easy. But it's lonely.
>
> Virginia Schwab, *The Archived*

The hatred that clown @krauthammer has for me is unbelievable—causes him to lie when many others say Trump easily won debate.

Tweet, August 7, 2015

> A false argument should be refuted, not named. That's the basic idea behind freedom of speech. Arguments by name-calling, rather than truth and light, can generally be presumed fraudulent.
>
> Ann Coulter

If Hillary Clinton can't satisfy her husband what makes her think she can satisfy America?

A tweet retweeted and subsequently deleted by Trump, April 16, 2015

> Yes, we praise women over 40 for a multitude of reasons. Unfortunately, it's not reciprocal. For every stunning, smart, well-coiffed, hot woman over 40, there is a bald, paunchy relic in yellow pants making a fool of himself with some 22-year old waitress. Ladies, I apologize. For all those men who say, "Why buy the cow when you can get the milk for free?", here's an update for you. Nowadays 80% of women are against marriage. Why? Because women realize it's not worth buying an entire pig just to get a little sausage!
>
> Andy Rooney

Russia, if you're listening, I hope you're able to find the 30,000 emails that are missing. I think you will probably be rewarded mightily by our press.

Calling on the Russian government to hack into and spy on Hillary Clinton's emails, July 27, 2016

> A nation can survive its fools, and even the ambitious. But it cannot survive treason from within. An enemy at the gates is less formidable, for he is known and carries his banner openly. But the traitor moves amongst those within the gate freely, his sly whispers rustling through all the alleys, heard in the very halls of government itself.
>
> Marcus Tullius Cicero

His father was with Lee Harvey Oswald prior to Oswald's being—you know, shot. I mean, the whole thing is ridiculous. What is this, right prior to his being shot, and nobody even brings it up. They don't even talk about that. That was reported, and nobody talks about it. I mean, what was he doing—what was he doing with Lee Harvey Oswald shortly before the death? Before the shooting? It's horrible.

Proclaiming that Senator Ted Cruz' father was involved with the plot to assassinate John F. Kennedy, Fox News interview, May 3, 2016

> A lie gets halfway around the world before the truth has a chance to get its pants on.
>
> Winston Churchill

Hillary Clinton . . . started the birther controversy. I finished it.

September 16, 2016

> If you tell the truth, you don't have to remember anything.
>
> Mark Twain

I think the only card she has is the women's card. She has got nothing else going. Frankly, if Hillary Clinton were a man, I don't think she would get 5 percent of the vote. And the beautiful thing is women don't like her, okay?

April 26, 2016

> Why do people say "grow some balls"? Balls are weak and sensitive. If you wanna be tough, grow a vagina. Those things can take a pounding.
>
> Sheng Wang

[W]e're bringing it from 1 percent up to 4 percent. And I actually think we can go higher than 4 percent. I think you can go to 5 percent or 6 percent.

October presidential debate with Hillary Clinton

> Do you really think you can do all that bullshit you just said?
>
> Captain Stephen Hiller, played by Will Smith, *Independence Day*, 1996

I actually think this election is going to be about competence. I'm a very competent person, okay. . . . Competence is going to be the biggest issue. They want to see somebody that's super competent, and that's me.

The Economist *interview, September 3, 2015*

> But then acting is all about faking. We're all very good at faking things that we have no competence with.
>
> John Cleese

The LGBT community, the gay community, the lesbian community—they are so much in favor of what I've been saying over the last three or four days. Ask the gays what they think and what they do, in, not only Saudi Arabia, but many of these countries, and then you tell me—who's your friend, Donald Trump or Hillary Clinton?

June 15, 2016

> "Civil rights groups to sue over Trump's plan for transgender military ban"
>
> *The Guardian*, August 5, 2017

Part of the problem and part of the reason it takes so long [to kick out protesters] is nobody wants to hurt each other anymore.

Campaign rally, St. Louis, Missouri, March 11, 2016

> There are more pleasant things to do than beat up people.
>
> Muhammad Ali

I've seen numbers of 24 percent. I actually saw a number of 42 percent unemployment. Forty-two percent. 5.3 percent unemployment—that is the biggest joke there is in this country. The unemployment rate is probably 20 percent, but I will tell you, you have some great economists that will tell you it's a 30, 32. And the highest I've heard so far is 42 percent.

Trying to pin down the unemployment rate, Sept. 28, 2015. Trump got it wrong on all counts.

> They are simply numbers and cannot thus be right or wrong. . . . What I trust that I am saying is that all numbers are by their nature correct. Well, except for Pi, of course. I can't be doing with Pi. Gives me a headache just thinking about it, going on and on and on and on and on.
>
> Neil Gaiman, *Anansi Boys*

I'm the most successful person ever to run for president. I mean, off the record, Ross Perot isn't successful like me. Romney was—I have a Gucci store that's worth more money than Romney.

June 1, 2015

> And, for an instant, she stared directly into those soft blue eyes and knew, with an instinctive mammalian certainty, that the exceedingly rich were no longer even remotely human.
>
> William Gibson, *Count Zero*

I think you'd have riots. I think you'd have riots. I'm representing many, many millions of people. In many cases first-time voters. . . . If you disenfranchise those people? And you say, well, I'm sorry, you're 100 votes short, even though the next one is 500 votes short? I think you'd have problems like you've never seen before. I wouldn't lead it, but I think bad things will happen.

Explaining what will happen if he's denied the Republican nomination in a contested convention, March 16, 2016

> What is most important of this grand experiment, the United States? Not the election of the first president but the election of its second president. The peaceful transition of power is what will separate this country from every other country in the world.
>
> George Washington

Do you know that Hillary Clinton was a birther? She wanted those records and fought like hell. People forgot. Did you know John McCain was a birther?

CNN interview, July 9, 2015

> Fact is, all lies, all evil deeds, they stink. You can cover them up for a while, but they don't go away.
>
> Dalton Russell, in the movie *Inside Man*, 2016

I always wanted to get the Purple Heart. This was much easier.

Campaign rally in Virginia, where a Trump supporter gave him his Purple Heart, August 2, 2016

> They wrote in the old days that it is sweet and fitting to die for one's country. But in modern war, there is nothing sweet nor fitting in your dying. You will die like a dog for no good reason.
>
> Ernest Hemingway

I'm the only one on this stage that said, "Do not go into Iraq. Do not attack Iraq." Nobody else on this stage said that. And I said it loud and strong.

Republican primary debate, South Carolina, February 13, 2016

> Yeah, I guess so.
>
> Donald Trump, interview with Howard Stern, 2002, when asked about whether he supported the Iraq War

If I win I am going to instruct my attorney general to get a special prosecutor to look into your situation—there has never been so many lies and so much deception.

Trump threatened Hillary Clinton with prosecution if he wins the election, October 2016 presidential debate.

> I believe the root of all evil is abuse of power.
>
> Patricia Cornwell

FBI director said Crooked Hillary compromised our national security. No charges. Wow! #RiggedSystem

Tweet, July 6, 2016

> Two things form the bedrock of any open society—freedom of expression and rule of law. If you don't have those things, you don't have a free country.
>
> Salman Rushdie

I'm speaking with myself, number one, because I have a very good brain and I've said a lot of things.

Answering a question about who his foreign policy advisors are, Morning Joe, *March 16, 2016*

> One advantage of talking to yourself is that you know at least somebody's listening.
>
> Franklin P. Jones

Many of the thugs that attacked the peaceful Trump supporters in San Jose were illegals. They burned the American flag and laughed at police.

Tweet, June 4, 2016

Peeta opens his mouth for the first bite without hesitation. He swallows, then frowns slightly. "They're very sweet."

"Yes they're sugar berries. My mother makes jam from them. Haven't you've ever had them before?" I say, poking the next spoonful in his mouth.

"No," he says, almost puzzled. "But they taste familiar. Sugar berries?"

"Well, you can't get them in the market much, they only grow wild," I say. Another mouthful goes down. Just one more to go.

"They're sweet as syrup," he says, taking the last spoonful. "Syrup." His eyes widen as he realizes the truth. I clamp my hand over his mouth and nose hard, forcing him to swallow instead of spit. He tries to make himself vomit the stuff up, but it's too late, he's already losing consciousness. Even as he fades away, I can see in his eyes what I've done is unforgivable.

I sit back on my heels and look at him with a mixture of sadness and satisfaction. A stray berry stains his chin and I wipe it away. "Who can't lie, Peeta?" I say, even though he can't hear me."

Suzanne Collins, *The Hunger Games*

Many people are saying that the Iranians killed the scientist who helped the U.S. because of Hillary Clinton's hacked emails.

Tweet, Aug 8, 2016

> These big falsehoods are different. They are like a neutron bomb. They just take over the discussion and obliterate a lot of other things that we should be discussing.
>
> Bill Adair, creator of PolitiFact, which won a Pulitzer Prize in 2009

Hillary Clinton is a bigot who sees people of color only as votes, not as human beings worthy of a better future.

Campaign rally in Jackson, Mississippi, August 24, 2016

> All my life, I have been taught to take the high road, and never to dignify salacious or false accusations. And I have been taught never, never to lie. Not only do I never lie, I never respond to lies, no matter how vicious, no matter how hurtful.
>
> Paula Abdul

[Hillary Clinton]'s being so protected. She could walk into this arena right now and shoot somebody with 20,000 people watching, right smack in the middle of the heart and she wouldn't be prosecuted, okay?

Campaign rally in Pensacola, Florida, September 9, 2016

> Any intelligent fool can make things bigger, more complex, and more violent. It takes a touch of genius—and a lot of courage to move in the opposite direction.
>
> Ernst F. Schumacher

Do people notice Hillary is copying my airplane rallies—she puts the plane behind her like I have been doing from the beginning.

Tweet, September 20, 2016

> For me, it is far better to grasp the Universe as it really is than to persist in delusion, however satisfying and reassuring.
>
> Carl Sagan, *The Demon-Haunted World: Science as a Candle in the Dark*

Here she is, in public, pretending not to hate Catholics.

Talking about Hillary Clinton, Al Smith dinner, a fundraiser for Catholic charities, October 20, 2016. Trump was booed.

> Anyone who thinks sitting in church can make you a Christian must also think that sitting in a garage can make you a car.
>
> Garrison Keillor

Vladimir Putin said today about Hillary and Dems: "In my opinion, it is humiliating. One must be able to lose with dignity." So true!

Tweet, December 24, 2016

> Democracy must be something more than two wolves and a sheep voting on what to have for dinner.
>
> James Bovard, *Lost Rights: The Destruction of American Liberty*

Other Domestic Issues

Sometimes, we can pin Trump down on the issues. This doesn't happen often because he speaks with broad-stroke adjectives to describe his positions rather than delving into the rich complexities of policy. Trump paints problems as a "disgrace" and promises "tremendous" change without ever saying exactly what he cares about.

Often, Trump changes his position like wind changing direction before a storm.

Trump has called China a currency manipulator, and un-called them that. He's claimed that NATO is obsolete, and then peddled backward.

Within the same sentence, Trump's able to take contradictory positions, as he did with guns schools: "I'm not advocating guns in classrooms, but remember, in some cases . . . trained teachers should be able to have guns in classrooms."

On healthcare, Trump has called for "repeal and replace" of Obamacare, pure repeal, and, once neither repeal and replace or repeal passed in Congress, Trump called for letting Obamacare fizzle away. During the campaign, Trump insisted, "We're going to have insurance for everybody. There was a philosophy in some circles that if you can't pay for it, you don't get it. That's not going to happen with us."

On immigration, deportations, and the wall, Trump has wandered all over the issue landscape. Finally, Trump threw up his hands when asked if there would ever be a path to citizenship: "I'm not ruling out anything. We're going to make that decision into the future. Okay?"

Trump's vacillated between the extreme barring of all Muslims from entering the United States to "[W]e have a serious problem, and it's a temporary ban—it hasn't been called for yet, nobody's done it, this is just a suggestion until we find out what's going on."

Trump's spoken out against raising the minimum wage, but he also tweeted: "Goofy Elizabeth Warren lied when she says I want to abolish the Federal Minimum Wage. See media—asking for increase!"

Trump opposed the H-1B program, which brings skilled workers to the United States. Then, during a debate, he said, "I am all in favor of keeping these talented people here so they can go to work in Silicon Valley."

On taxes, Trump is so all over the map that his positions are no more of a map than a divining rod is real tool for finding water. "I do, I do, including myself. I do," is how Trump responded to a question at a town hall meeting about whether he thought taxes should be raised on the wealthy. Trump's also said there should be tax cuts across all income brackets. As he's done before, he's even offered contradictory positions within the same thought: "The middle class has to be protected. The rich is probably going to end up paying more. And business might have to pay a little bit more. But we're giving a massive business tax cut." Say what?

Do you need clarification on Trump's tax plans? Here it is in his own words: "If I increase it on the wealthy, that means they're still going to be paying less than they're paying now. I'm not increasing it from this point, I'm talking about increasing from my tax proposal." Maybe this makes sense to a six-year-old.

When we are able to pin down Trump's policies, they're far to the right of center. He's against a woman's right to choose. He's against transgender people serving in the military. He's against affordable healthcare (his rhetoric aside). He's pro-gun.

I would bring back waterboarding. And I'd bring back a hell of a lot worse than waterboarding.

Republican primary debate in New Hampshire, February 6, 2016

> Under torture you are as if under the dominion of those grasses that produce visions. Everything you have heard told, everything you have read returns to your mind, as if you were being transported, not toward heaven, but toward hell. Under torture you say not only what the inquisitor wants, but also what you imagine might please him, because a bond (this, truly, diabolical) is established between you and him. . . . These things I know, Ubertino; I also have belonged to those groups of men who believe they can produce the truth with white-hot iron. Well, let me tell you, the white heat of truth comes from another flame.
>
> Umberto Eco, *The Name of the Rose*

When you see these towns and when you see these thugs being thrown into the back of a paddy wagon, you just see them thrown in, rough, and I said, "Please don't be too nice."

Like when you guys put somebody in the car and you're protecting their head, you know, the way you put their hand over, like, don't hit their head and they've just killed somebody, don't hit their head, I said, 'You can take the hand away, okay?'"

Speech to law enforcement officers on Long Island, July 28, 2017, in which Trump said it was okay to rough up prisoners.

> The clearest way to show what the rule of law means to us in everyday life is to recall what has happened when there is no rule of law.
>
> Dwight D. Eisenhower

Don't tell me it doesn't work—torture works. Half these guys [say], "torture doesn't work." Believe me, it works.

Campaign event South Carolina, February 17, 2016

> The Dead Hand, yeah, it was, like, seminal, but tame by today's standards. Violet, for instance, did not get her intestines ripped out. There wasn't any torture, nobody's liver got fried in a pan, there wasn't any gang rape. So what's the fun of that?
>
> Margaret Atwood, *Stone Mattress: Nine Tales*

People said I want to go and buy debt and default on debt, and I mean, these people are crazy. This is the United States government. First of all, you never have to default because you print the money. I hate to tell you, okay? So there's never a default.

CNN interview, May 10, 2016

> If printing money helped the economy, then counterfeiting should be legal.
>
> Brian Wesbury

Last quarter, it was just announced our gross domestic product—a sign of strength, right? But not for us. It was below zero. Whoever heard of this? It's never below zero. Our labor participation rate was the worst since 1978. But think of it, GDP below zero, horrible labor participation rate. And our real unemployment is anywhere from 18 to 20 percent. Don't believe the 5.6. Don't believe it.

That's right. A lot of people up there can't get jobs. They can't get jobs, because there are no jobs, because China has our jobs and Mexico has our jobs. They all have jobs.

But the real number, the real number is anywhere from 18 to 19 and maybe even 21 percent, and nobody talks about it, because it's a statistic that's full of nonsense.

Speech announcing his candidacy for president, June 16, 2015

> I never made a mistake in my life; at least, never one that I couldn't explain away afterwards.
>
> Rudyard Kipling, *Under The Deodars*

[Gang members] don't want to use guns because it's too fast and it's not painful enough, so they'll take a young, beautiful girl, 16, 15 and others and they slice them and dice them with a knife because they want them to go through excruciating pain before they die, and these are the animals that we've been protecting for so long.

Well, they're not being protected any longer, folks. And that is why my administration is launching a nationwide crackdown on sanctuary cities.

Speech in Youngstown, Ohio, July 25, 2017

> It is by a thorough knowledge of the whole subject that [people] are enabled to judge correctly of the past and to give a proper direction to the future.
>
> James Monroe

Are we going to take down the statue? Cause he was a major slave owner. Are we going to take down his statue? So you know what? It's fine. You are changing history, you're changing culture.

Press conference, August 16, 2017. Talking about Charlottesville and the question of statues of Confederate generals.

> If you are neutral in situations of injustice, you have chosen the side of the oppressor. If an elephant has its foot on the tail of a mouse and you say that you are neutral, the mouse will not appreciate your neutrality.
>
> Desmond Tutu

I am pleased to inform you that I have just granted a full Pardon to 85 year old American patriot Sheriff Joe Arpaio. He kept Arizona safe!

Tweet, August 26, 2017. Arizona Sheriff Joe Arpaio engaged in systematic racial profiling and was convicted of contempt of court for violating a judge's order barring him from detaining anyone simply because he thought they were an illegal immigrant. Arpaio is also a birther.

> This is his pardon, purchas'd by such sin
> For which the pardoner himself is in.
>
> William Shakespeare, *Measure for Measure*, Act 4, Scene 2

And by the way, under the Trump administration, you'll be saying "Merry Christmas" again when you go shopping. Believe me. "Merry Christmas."

Speech at Boy Scout Jamboree, Glen Jean, West Virginia July 24, 2017

> Summer, after all, is a time when wonderful things can happen to quiet people. For those few months, you're not required to be who everyone thinks you are, and that cut-grass smell in the air and the chance to dive into the deep end of a pool give you a courage you don't have the rest of the year. You can be grateful and easy, with no eyes on you, and no past. Summer just opens the door and lets you out.
>
> Deb Caletti, *Honey, Baby, Sweetheart*

I think you need clarity with financing. I do think this. I think that you need clarity, you have to be able to see who's giving. You don't even see that any . . . you don't even see that. Because some of these things they put up on there, nobody knows who they are, where they are coming from etc etc. You need clarity. You have to be able to see, I don't like restriction but I do want clarity.

Responding to the question, "Would a President Trump pass new laws on campaign finance?" The Economist *interview, September 3, 2017*

The story of Yoshitsune and the Thousand Cherry Trees was both simple and complicated. Simple in that things never change: people consistently jealous or secretive or brave-hearted. As for the rest, it all came down to a series of misunderstandings, the type that could happen to anyone, really. You assume that the sushi bucket is full of gold coins, but instead it's got Kokingo's head in it. You think you know everything about your faithful follower, but it turns out that he's actually an orphaned fox who can change his shape at will. It was he who spoke my favorite line of the evening, five words that perfectly conveyed just how enchanting and full of surprises this Kabuki play really is: "that drum is my father."

David Sedaris

Under my proposal, it's the biggest tax cut by far, of any candidate by far. But I'm not under the illusion that that's going to pass. They're going to come to me. They're going to want to raise it for the rich. Frankly, they're going to want to raise it for the rich more than anybody else. But the middle class has to be protected. The rich is probably going to end up paying more. And business might have to pay a little bit more. But we're giving a massive business tax cut.

NBC with Chuck Todd, 2016

> But Noodynaady's actual ingrate tootle is of come into the garner mauve and thy nice are stores of morning and buy me a bunch of iodines.
>
> James Joyce, *Finnegans Wake*

[The Trans-Pacific Partnership] is done and pushed by special interests who want to rape our country. That's what it is, too. It's a harsh word. It's a rape of our country.

Ohio campaign rally, June 28, 2016

> A day will come when there will be no battlefields, but markets opening to commerce and minds opening to ideas.
>
> Victor Hugo

I would do stop-and-frisk. I think you have to. We did it in New York, it worked incredibly well and you have to be proactive and, you know, you really help people sort of change their mind automatically.

Fox News interview, September 21, 2016

> She said, "Sheriff how come you to let crime get so out of hand in your county?" Sounded like a fair question I reckon. Maybe it was a fair question. Anyway I told her, I said, "It starts when you begin to overlook bad manners. Any time you quit hearin Sir and Mam the end is pretty much in sight."
>
> Cormac McCarthy, *No Country for Old Men*

Well, if that would happen, because I am pro-life, and I will be appointing pro-life judges, I would think that that will go back to the individual states. If we put another two or perhaps three justice on, that's really what's going to be. That'll happen automatically, in my opinion, because I am putting pro-life justices on the court. I will say this: It will go back to the states, and the states will then make a determination.

Third presidential debate, Oct 19, 2016, answering a question about whether he wants Roe v. Wade *overturned.*

> Seventy-seven percent of anti-abortion leaders are men. 100% of them will never be pregnant.
>
> Planned Parenthood

I'm going to create tremendous jobs. And we're bringing GDP from, really, 1 percent [growth rate], which is what it is now, and if she got in, it will be less than zero. But we're bringing it from 1 percent up to 4 percent. And I actually think we can go higher than 4 percent. I think you can go to 5 percent or 6 percent. And if we do, you don't have to bother asking your question, because we will have created a tremendous economic machine once again, the likes of which we haven't seen in many decades. And people will again go back to work, and we'll have companies that will grow and expand and start from new.

Presidential debate, Las Vegas, October 19, 2016

> Innovation carried out by immigrants also has the potential to increase the productivity of natives, very likely raising economic growth per capita. In short, the prospects for long run economic growth in the United States would be considerably dimmed without the contributions of high-skilled immigrants.
>
> National Academy of Sciences, "The Economic and Fiscal Consequences of Immigration," 2016

We are in a bubble right now. The Fed, by keeping interest rates at this level, is doing political things. The Fed is being more political than Secretary Clinton.

Presidential debate, September 27, 2016

> Liberalism is, I think, resurgent. One reason is that more and more people are so painfully aware of the alternative.
>
> John Kenneth Galbraith, *The New York Times*, October 8, 1989

It's a very rough system. It's an archaic system. It's really a bad thing for the country.

Donald Trump talking about the Constitution's system of checks and balances during a Fox News interview on Trump's 99th day in office.

> The White House isn't the place to learn how to deal with international crisis, the balance of power, war and peace, and the economic future of the next generation.
>
> Joe Biden

I'm a good Christian. If I become president, we're going to be saying "Merry Christmas" at every store . . . You can leave "Happy Holidays" at the corner.

Speech in Burlington, Iowa, October 21, 2015

> The year showed me beyond a doubt that everyone practices cafeteria religion . . . But the important lesson was this: there's nothing wrong with choosing. Cafeterias aren't bad per se . . . The key is in choosing the right dishes. You need to pick the nurturing ones (compassion), the healthy ones (love thy neighbor), not the bitter ones.
>
> A.J. Jacobs, *The Year of Living Biblically: One Man's Humble Quest to Follow the Bible as Literally as Possible*

We're going to make a dynamic economy from what we have right now. We're going to bring jobs back from Japan, we're going to bring jobs back from China, we're going to bring, frankly, jobs back from Mexico where, as you probably saw, Nabisco is leaving Chicago with one of their biggest plants, and they're moving it to Mexico. We're going to bring jobs and manufacturing back. We're going to cut costs. We're going to save Social Security, and we're going to save Medicare.

GOP debate, Oct 28, 2015

> It's better not to make a promise than to make one you can't keep.
>
> V.C. Andrews, *Pearl in the Mist*

In Pennsylvania, two weeks ago, they opened a mine, the first mine that was opened in decades. Opened a mine. And you know all the people that were saying the mining jobs? Well we picked up 45,000 mining jobs in a very short period of time, and everybody was saying, well, you won't get any mining jobs. We picked up 45,000 mining jobs.

July 18, 2017. The White House did not provide any evidence of this 45,000 jobs number.

> I feel like a man standing at the mouth of an old mine-shaft that is full of cave-ins waiting to happen, standing there and saying goodbye to the daylight.
>
> Stephen King, *It*

I would use the debt limit. I want to be unpredictable, because, you know, we need unpredictability. Everything is so predictable with our country.

Answering a question about whether he would use the debt limit as a bargaining chip to get spending cuts, Fox News Sunday, Oct 18, 2015.

> Some scientists claim that hydrogen, because it is so plentiful, is the basic building block of the universe. I dispute that. I say there is more stupidity than hydrogen, and that is the basic building block of the universe.
>
> Frank Zappa

We need to lower the U.S. corporate tax rate from 39 percent to zero. America's corporate tax rate is the second highest on the planet. The international average is 26 percent. How can we expect companies to hire American workers and locate their business in America when our government taxes them at exorbitant rates for doing so? That's crazy. I want to encourage American companies to stay here and hire American workers, and I want foreign companies to relocate their businesses to the United States and create jobs here. We are the greatest country on planet earth—the world's companies want to be here. A zero percent corporate tax would create an unprecedented jobs boom. Millions of jobs would materialize.

Trump, Time to Get Tough

> I like to pay taxes. With them, I buy civilization.
>
> Oliver Wendell Holmes Jr.

Good luck to everybody.

August 25, 2017, responding to a reporter's question, " "Do you have a message for the people of Texas?" before Category 4 Hurricane Harvey struck Texas.

> Shallow men believe in luck or in circumstance. Strong men believe in cause and effect.
>
> Ralph Waldo Emerson

I love capitalism enough to protect it. There has to be a level playing field where everyone can compete fairly. The guy swinging a hammer all day shouldn't have the government reaching in his pocket and handing his taxes to Obama's big shot donors. It's wrong and unfair.

Trump, Time to Get Tough, *2011*

> At least 60 lawsuits, along with hundreds of liens, judgments, and other government filings reviewed by the USA TODAY NETWORK, document people who have accused Trump and his businesses of failing to pay them for their work. Among them: a dishwasher in Florida. A glass company in New Jersey. A carpet company. A plumber. Painters. Forty-eight waiters. Dozens of bartenders and other hourly workers at his resorts and clubs, coast to coast. Real estate brokers who sold his properties. And, ironically, several law firms that once represented him in these suits and others.
>
> Trump's companies have also been cited for 24 violations of the Fair Labor Standards Act since 2005 for failing to pay overtime or minimum wage, according to U.S. Department of Labor data.
>
> *USA Today*, June 9, 2016

It's called priming the pump. You know, if you don't do that, you're never going to bring your taxes down. Now, if we get the health-care [bill through Congress], this is why, you know a lot of people said, "Why isn't he going with taxes first, that's his wheelhouse?" Well, hey look, I convinced many people over the last two weeks, believe me, many Congressmen, to go with it. And they're great people, but one of the great things about getting health care is that we will be saving, I mean anywhere from $400 billion to $90 billion . . .

That all goes into tax reduction. Tremendous savings.

The Economist question: But beyond that it's OK if the tax plan increases the deficit?

It is okay, because it won't increase it for long. You may have two years where you'll . . . you understand the expression "prime the pump"?

The Economist: Yes.

We have to prime the pump.

The Economist: It's very Keynesian.

We're the highest-taxed nation in the world. Have you heard that expression before, for this particular type of an event?

The Economist: Priming the pump?

Yeah, have you heard it?

The Economist: Yes.

Have you heard that expression used before? Because I haven't heard it. I mean, I just . . . I came up with it a couple of days ago and I thought it was good. It's what you have to do.

The Economist: It's . . .

Yeah, what you have to do is you have to put something in before you can get something out.

Interview with the The Economist, *May 11, 2017, in which Trump claims he invented the economic term "priming the pump." According to Merriam-Webster dictionary, "priming the pump" was used as far back as the early 19th century.*

> The easiest thing in the world is to convince yourself that you are right. As one grows older, this is easier still.
>
> Robert Ludlum, *The Bourne Identity*

I just think that the booming economy that we create by my plan would keep the money here because it's incentive. They're going to want to be where the action is. They're going to want to be where the good economy is. And they move their money around, hey, including me. You move your money around where the action is, and now it's a real world economy. But this country would be booming. We'd have no debt. It would be unbelievable

April 2011

> Bullshit is the glue that binds us as a nation.
>
> George Carlin

There has been a big push to develop alternative forms of energy—so-called green energy—from renewable sources. That's a big mistake. To begin with, the whole push for renewable energy is being driven by the wrong motivation, the mistaken belief that global climate change is being caused by carbon emissions. If you don't buy that—and I don't—then what we have is really just an expensive way of making the tree-huggers feel good about themselves.

Crippled America

> Here is your country. Cherish these natural wonders, cherish the natural resources, cherish the history and romance as a sacred heritage, for your children and your children's children. Do not let selfish men or greedy interests skin your country of its beauty, its riches or its romance.
>
> Theodore Roosevelt

The Presidency

Speaking at a campaign rally in Youngstown, Ohio in July 2017, Trump compared his presidency to Abraham Lincoln's. (Yes, I know, the campaign ended half a year earlier, but Trump is a fish in water when he's speaking to adoring, fawning crowds.) Trump said—are you ready for this?

> *Sometimes, they say, "He doesn't act presidential." And I say, "Hey look—great schools, smart guy—it's so easy to act presidential. But that's not going to get it done. . . . With the exception of the late, great Abraham Lincoln, I can be more presidential than any president that's ever held this office. That I can tell you. It's real easy."*

Never mind the incoherence of Trump's remarks. Trump believes that by merely occupying the Oval Office, he's automatically elevated to greatness. The wish to be memorialized on Mt. Rushmore along with George Washington, Thomas Jefferson, Theodore Roosevelt, and Abraham Lincoln swirls in the delusions of his mind. Trump joked—but it wasn't a joke—in Youngstown, Ohio in July 2017, "I'd ask whether or not you think I will someday be on Mount Rushmore, but here's the problem: If I did it joking, totally joking, having fun, the fake news media will say, 'He believes he should be on Mount Rushmore' . . ." So I won't say it, okay? I won't say it."

Trump's presidency is an act of self-deception. It's also an act of do-nothing. (Though I suppose Trump considers tweeting to be working.) As I write *Trump Corrected*, eight months into Trump's presidency, his list of major legislation has zero items on it. He recently took a seventeen-day vacation at his private golf courses in New Jersey. He has spent forty days playing golf. During his first six months, twelve senior staffers resigned, including Trump's press secretary, National Security Advisor, and Chief of Staff.

Confusion and disarray are such potent forces inside the White House that Trump felt compelled to tweet, "No WH chaos!"

James Fallows asks, via Twitter, "If you're not worried about a man in Trump's temperamental condition becoming commander-in-chief, then—tell me why you're not!"

That's a great question. I'll add to that you should also be worried about Trump's love of lying, misogynistic behavior, and his cruel contempt for anyone he perceives as his enemy.

One of Trump's first lies as president was when he claimed, "The President of Taiwan CALLED ME today to wish me congratulations on winning the presidency."

(Why would he even bother to lie about such a triviality as who called whom?)

When a former Miss Universe, Alicia Machado, became a campaign issue, Trump urged people to check out her (non-existent) sex tape, claiming, "Crooked Hillary was duped and used by my worst Miss U. Hillary floated her as an 'angel' without checking her past, which is terrible!" Great. We have a president who urges people to check out the sex tapes of his opponents.

Trump can't tolerate Saturday Night Live's satire of him: "Just tried watching Saturday Night Live—unwatchable! Totally biased, not funny and the Baldwin impersonation just can't get any worse. Sad," he tweeted. Trump's ego and pride are made of tissue paper. He's going to have an impossible time as the most criticized person in the world, the President of the United States.

Trump is frighteningly susceptible to fringe conspiracy theories. Until recently, he was the biggest booster of the wildly ignorant and outlandish claim that Barack Obama wasn't born in the United States.

Trump thought that it was okay to barge in on Miss Universe contestants in their changing room—while they were naked. Trump said, "I'll go backstage before a show, and everyone's getting dressed and ready and everything else. And you know, no men are anywhere. And I'm allowed to go in because I'm the owner of the pageant. And therefore I'm inspecting it."

This is the man who sits in the Oval Office.

And now, as President, Trump has accomplished little—little positive that is. He's added fuel to American white supremacists and neo-Nazis' fire. Trump has strained America's relationship with South Korea—when North Korea nuclear weapons capability has grown. And not just

South Korea: Trump doesn't care about alliances. Here's a two-tweet thrashing he gave Germany in March 2017: Despite what you have heard from the FAKE NEWS, I had a GREAT meeting with German Chancellor Angela Merkel. Nevertheless, Germany owes vast sums of money to NATO & the United States must be paid more for the powerful, and very expensive, defense it provides to Germany!" Trump has banned transgender American from serving in the military. Trump's overturned the Deferred Action for Childhood Arrivals. He lies every day. Really.

Trump outputs information in 140 characters, but unfortunately that's the maximum size of information and analysis he can comprehend.

I find the job very natural for me. I find—it's a very big job obviously, there's no job big like this. No job is important like this. But I think some of the—I just think it's something that works for me, it feels very natural to me.

And all I said, the job, it is, it's a difficult job but it's a job that I find to be—I love doing it. I love helping people. Mike [Pence] is doing a fantastic job. He fits it so well. I mean we have a great team, he and I guess, they say we're somewhat opposite and that works to be a very good combination.

Time *magazine interview, May 11, 2017*

> Stupidity is also a gift of God, but one mustn't misuse it.
>
> Pope John Paul II

Have a good time.

Said to hurricane Harvey evacuees living in shelters. People who may have lost their homes, business, friends, and family, September 1, 2017.

> One thing you can't hide is when you're crippled inside.
>
> John Lennon

That White House is a real dump.

Talking with golfing buddies at the Trump National Bedminster golf club, Golf Magazine, *August 1, 2017*

> In the evening, when Michelle and the girls have gone to bed, I sometimes walk down the hall to a room Abraham Lincoln used as his office. It contains an original copy of the Gettysburg address, written in Lincoln's own hand.
>
> I linger on those few words that have helped define our American experiment: "A new nation, conceived in liberty, and dedicated to the proposition that all men are created equal."
>
> Barack Obama, 2013

Boy Scout values are American values. And great Boy Scouts become great, great Americans. As the Scout law says, a Scout is trustworthy, loyal. We could use some more loyalty, I could tell you that.

Speech at Boy Scout Jamboree, Glen Jean, West Virginia July 24, 2017

> Patriotism is supporting your country all the time and your government when it deserves it.
>
> Mark Twain

> I've done a lot with Mike [Pence] where we have a meeting in the [Roosevelt Room], we'll have a lot of different people, labor unions, workers. . . . We had Harley Davidson up. I'll say anybody ever see the Oval Office? Nobody's ever said they've seen the Oval Office. President Obama was different. He didn't, not a lot of people invited in. Me, I invite people in. . . .
>
> And it means something, the Oval Office. It means something to them. I'm telling you I've had big people, some of the biggest business people, you've seen it. They go in they're like, they can't believe it. And I've seen them cry. It's weird.

Time *magazine interview, May 11, 2017*

> The haggardness of poverty is everywhere seen contrasted with the sleekness of wealth, the exhorted labour of some compensating for the idleness of others, wretched hovels by the side of stately colonnades, the rags of indigence blended with the ensigns of opulence; in a word, the most useless profusion in the midst of the most urgent wants.
>
> Jean-Baptiste Say

He told me off the record he may go [to] $30 billion—$30 billion—think of this. But he told me that off the record, so I promised I wouldn't tell anybody.

Remarks about Foxconn building a factory in Wisconsin, during a press conference, August 1, 2017

> Don't trust people who tell you other people's secrets.
>
> Dan Howell

No WH chaos.

From a tweet, July 31, 2017. "WH" stands for White House. Trump was probably referring to the recent resignations of his Chief of Staff, Press Secretary, and Communications Director (the latter lasted only ten days).

> Judge Randolph: [to Kaffee from the judge's bench] Consider yourself in contempt!
>
> Kaffee: Colonel Jessup, did you order the Code Red?
>
> Judge Randolph: You don't have to answer that question!
>
> Col. Jessup: I'll answer the question!
>
> Col. Jessup: You want answers?

Kaffee: I think I'm entitled to.

Col. Jessep: You want answers?

Kaffee: I WANT THE TRUTH!

Col. Jessup: YOU CAN'T HANDLE THE TRUTH!

A Few Good Men, 1992, movie written by Aaron Sorkin, starring Tom Cruise, Jack Nicholson, and Demi Moore

We pay for Obama's travel so he can fundraise millions so Democrats can run on lies. Then we pay for his golf.

Tweet, October 15, 2014

You know how I can tell if a 17-year-old girl is lying? When her mouth moves.

Judge Judy, 1996

I have a great heart for the folks we are talking about, a great love for them.

Talking about the Dreamers, immigrant children who are (or were) allowed to remain in the United States. Trump ordered

the Deferred Action for Childhood Arrivals, DACA program, through which they could stay in the United States, ended. September 5, 2017. No love there at all.

> Deliberate cruelty is unforgivable.
>
> Blanche Dubois in Tennessee Williams's *A Streetcar Named Desire*

"One of the most effective press conferences I've ever seen!" says Rush Limbaugh. Many agree.Yet FAKE MEDIA calls it differently! Dishonest

Tweet, February 18, 2017

> Avoid having your ego so close to your position that when your position falls, your ego goes with it.
>
> Colin Powell

You know what's interesting, I'm getting very good marks in foreign policy. People would not think of me in that light. I'm just saying, and you read the same things I read. I'm getting As and A+s on foreign policy. And nobody thought about it.

Time *magazine interview, May 11, 2017*

> A delusion is something that people believe in despite a total lack of evidence.
>
> Richard Dawkins

We need to be smart, vigilant and tough. We need the courts to give us back our rights. We need the Travel Ban as an extra level of safety!

Tweet, June 4, 2017

> Whatever government is not a government of laws, is a despotism, let it be called what it may.
>
> Daniel Webster

Sometimes they say, "He does not act presidential," and I say, "Hey, look. Great schools, smart guy, it's so easy to act presidential, but that's not going to get it done."

Speech in Youngstown, Ohio, July 25, 2017

> People do not wish to appear foolish; to avoid the appearance of foolishness, they are willing to remain actually fools.
>
> Alice Walker

And in the end he failed and he failed badly. Lost all of his money. He went personally bankrupt. And he was now much older. And I saw him at a cocktail party and it was very sad because the hottest people in New York were at this party. And I see sitting in the corner, was a little old man who was all by himself. Nobody was talking to him. I immediately recognized that that man was the once great William Levitt of Levittown.

And he said, "Donald, I lost my momentum. I lost my momentum." A word you never hear when you're talking about success.

He lost his momentum, meaning he took this period of time off long, years, and then when he got back, he didn't have the same momentum.

In life, I always tell this to people. You have to know whether or not you continue to have the momentum. And if you don't have it that's okay.

Speech at Boy Scout Jamboree, talking about real estate developer William Levitt, Glen Jean, West Virginia July, 24, 2017

> Be not careless in deeds, nor confused in words, nor rambling in thought.
>
> Marcus Aurelius

Well the one thing I would say—and I say this to people—I never realized how big it was. Everything's so [unintelligible] like, you know the orders are so massive. . . .

Number One, there's great responsibility. When it came time to, as an example, send out the 59 missiles, the Tomahawks in Syria. I'm saying to myself, "You know, this is more than just like, 79 [*sic]* missiles. This is death that's involved," because people could have been killed. This is risk that's involved, because if the missile goes off and goes in a city or goes in a civilian area—you know, the boats were hundreds of miles away—and if this missile goes off and lands in the middle of a town or a hamlet . . . every decision is much harder than you'd normally make.[unintelligible]. . . . This is involving death and life and so many things. . . . So it's far more responsibility. [unintelligible] . . . The financial cost of everything is so massive, every agency. This is thousands of times bigger, the United States, than the biggest company in the world. The second-largest company in the world is the Defence Department. The third-largest company in the world is Social Security. The fourth-largest—you know, you go down the list. . . .

It's massive. And every agency is, like, bigger than any company. So you know, I really just see the bigness of it all, but also the responsibility. And the human responsibility. You know, the human life that's involved in some of the decisions.

Answer to the question, "How do you feel like the office has changed you?" during an interview with the Associated Press, April 22, 2017.

> I know all those words, but that sentence makes no sense to me.
>
> Matt Groening

"Don't take vacations. What's the point? If you're not enjoying your work, you're in the wrong job."—Think Like A Billionaire

Tweet, November 20, 2012

> I don't count my sit-ups; I only start counting when it starts hurting because they're the only ones that count.
>
> Muhammad Ali

Make America Great Again

The hats and the slogans were catchy, clever, and ultimately successful. Donald J. Trump rode the magic carpet of "Make America Great Again" to the White House.

"Make America Great Again" is as sinister as it is clever. The slogan promises manufacturing and mining jobs that slipped away over the past decade. Never mind that many manufacturing jobs have come and gone, not because of immigration or trade policies, but because of technological advances. Think solar, natural gas, and wind energy, and you get the idea.

The slogan promised those who were receptive to its charms an America that's white, or at least whiter, again. It's a slogan that attracts white nationalists and racists. "Make America Great" again has at its core a strong anti-immigration component. It is about keeping non-English speaking, non-whites out of America.

Engraved on the Statue of Liberty, the symbol of America's openness toward immigrants is Emma Lazarus's' famous poem:

> *. . . Give me your tired, your poor,*
> *Your huddled masses, yearning to breathe free,*
> *The wretched refuse of your teeming shore,*
> *Send these, the homeless, tempest-tost to me,*
> *I lift my lamp beside the golden door.*

When asked about that poem during a press briefing on August 2, 2017, Stephen Miller, a senior policy advisor to Donald Trump, said the poem wasn't part of the original statue; it was added later. This is a popular refrain among white nationalists.

The foundation of Trump's "Make America Great Again" slogan is a dark, disturbed, weak and irresolute America. Trump's America is one where businesses can't succeed, where people can't find jobs, where immigrants are nightmarish weeds that suffocate true Americans. His speech accepting the Republican nomination for president was gloomy, like a page out of a dystopian novel: "Our convention occurs at a moment of crisis for our nation. . . . The attacks on our police, and the terrorism in our cities, threaten our very way of life. Any politician who does not grasp this danger is not fit to lead our country." Trump's speech was peppered with cheerless lines, like "America is far less safe—and the world is far less stable—than when Obama made the decision to put Hillary Clinton in charge of America's foreign policy," and it asserted that America had "lived through one international humiliation after another." Rather than inspire or uplift, Trump's inauguration speech painted America darkly: "For too long, a small group in our nation's capital has reaped the rewards of government while the people have borne the cost. Washington flourished, but the people did not share in its wealth. Politicians prospered, but the jobs left. And the factories closed."

Trump's words were perhaps the darkest of any Presidential inauguration address:

> *But for too many of our citizens, a different reality exists. Mothers and children trapped in poverty in our inner cities, rusted-out factories scattered like tombstones across the landscape of our nation, an education system flush with cash but which leaves our young and beautiful students deprived of all knowledge. And the crime, and the gangs, and the drugs that have stolen too many lives and robbed our country of so much unrealized potential. This American carnage stops right here and stops right now.*

Trump's path toward making America great again starts with a country that's anything but America.

Our country is in serious trouble. We don't have victories anymore. We used to have victories, but we don't have them. When was the last time anybody saw us beating, let's say China, in a trade deal? I beat China all the time. All the time.

Speech announcing his candidacy for president, June 2015

> America was not built on fear. America was built on courage, on imagination and an unbeatable determination to do the job at hand.
>
> Harry S. Truman

It's like in golf. A lot of people—I don't want this to sound trivial—but a lot of people are switching to these really long putters, very unattractive. It's weird. You see these great players with these really long putters, because they can't sink three-footers anymore. And, I hate it. I am a traditionalist. I have so many fabulous friends who happen to be gay, but I am a traditionalist.

The New York Times *interview, May 2011, talking about gay marriage*

> If you're not sure how you feel [about same-sex marriage], go and meet some of the families and see what they're looking for. Once you take it out of the caricature of what gay marriage is, and put

> it in the reality of family and what these folks are fighting for, it's really amazing.
>
> Whoopi Goldberg

I love the poorly educated.

Talking about the demographic groups that got him elected, February 2016

> Education is the most powerful weapon which you can use to change the world.
>
> Nelson Mandela

Last week a brand-new coal mine just opened in the state of Pennsylvania, first time in decades, decades.

June 21, 2017. The New York Times *reported that another coal mine opened in Pennsylvania in 2014.*

> Facts are stubborn things; and whatever may be our wishes, our inclinations, or the dictates of our passion, they cannot alter the state of facts and evidence.
>
> John Adams

According to the economists—who I'm not big believers in, but, nevertheless, this is what they're saying—that $24 trillion—we're very close—that's the point of no return. $24 trillion. We will be there soon. That's when we become Greece. That's when we become a country that's unsalvageable. And we're gonna be there very soon. We're gonna be there very soon.

Speech announcing his candidacy for President, June 16, 2015

> Cynicism masquerades as wisdom, but it is the farthest thing from it. Because cynics don't learn anything. Because cynicism is a self-imposed blindness, a rejection of the world because we are afraid it will hurt us or disappoint us.
>
> Stephen Colbert

I go to Washington and I see all these politicians, and I see the swamp. In fact it's not a good place—we should change it from the swamp to the cesspool or perhaps use the word sewer.

Speech at Boy Scout Jamboree, Glen Jean, West Virginia July 24, 2017

> And that's what innocence is. It's simple and trusting like a child, not judgmental and committed to one narrow point of view. If you are locked

into a pattern of thinking and responding, your creativity gets blocked. You miss the freshness and magic of the moment. Learn to be innocent again, and that freshness never fades.

Michael Jackson

More My first order as President was to renovate and modernize our nuclear arsenal. It is now far stronger and more powerful than ever before.

Tweet, August 9, 2017

What is it with you people? You think not getting caught in a lie is the same thing as telling the truth.

Robert Redford in *Three Days of the Condor*

Things have happened, having to do with many things including political correctness, where people are so worried about being politically correct that they are unable to function.

The Economist *interview, September 3, 2017*

Let's have some new cliches.

Samuel Goldwyn

I am the toughest guy. I will rebuild our military.... Nobody's going to mess with us.

Campaign rally, Mobile, Alabama August 21, 2015

> Every day we're told that we live in the greatest country on earth. And it's always stated as an undeniable fact: Leos are born between July 23 and August 22, fitted queen-size sheets measure sixty by eighty inches, and America is the greatest country on earth. Having grown up with this in our ears, it's startling to realize that other countries have nationalistic slogans of their own, none of which are "We're number two!"
>
> David Sedaris, *Me Talk Pretty One Day*

We're a very powerful nuclear country and so [is Russia]. I've been briefed. And I can tell you one thing about a briefing that we're allowed to say, because anybody that ever read the most basic book can say it, nuclear holocaust would be like no other.

February 15, 2017

> A nuclear war cannot be won and must never be fought. The only value in our two nations possessing nuclear weapons is to make sure they will

> never be used. But then would it not be better to do away with them entirely?
>
> Ronald Reagan, 1984 State of the Union address

The United States must greatly strengthen and expand its nuclear capability until such time as the world comes to its senses regarding nukes

Tweet, December 23, 2016

> The nuclear arms race is like two sworn enemies standing waist deep in gasoline, one with three matches, the other with five.
>
> Carl Sagan

I will have a military that's so strong and powerful, and so respected, we're not gonna have to nuke anybody. . . . It is highly, highly, highly, highly unlikely that I would ever be using them.

GQ *interview, November 2015*

> I want to say, and this is very important: at the end we lucked out. It was luck that prevented nuclear war. We came that close to nuclear war at the end. Rational individuals: Kennedy was rational; Khrushchev was rational; Castro was rational. Rational individuals came that close to total destruction of their societies. And that danger exists today.
>
> Robert McNamara on the Cuban Missile Crisis

The big problem this country has is being politically correct. I've been challenged by so many people, and I don't really have time for total political correctness, and to be honest with you, our country doesn't have time either. This country is in big trouble, we don't win anymore, we lose to China, we lose to Mexico, both in trade and at the border, we lose to everybody. And frankly, what I say, and oftentimes it's fun, we're kidding, we have a good time. What I say is what I say. And honestly Megyn, if you don't like it, I'm sorry. I've been very nice to you, although I could probably maybe not be based on the way you've treated me, but I wouldn't do that.

GOP debate, 2016

> Magic Mirror on the wall, who is the fairest one of all?
>
> Snow White and the Seven Dwarves, 1937

My opinion on the settlement of the Central Park Jogger case is that it's a disgrace. A detective close to the case, and who has followed it since 1989, calls it "the heist of the century." . . . Speak to the detectives on the case and try listening to the facts. These young men do not exactly have the pasts of angels.

Op-ed, New York Daily News, *June 21, 2014, about the Central Park jogger case. Five juvenile men, four black and one of Hispanic origin, were convicted of raping and assaulting a female jogger in Central Park in 1989. Their convictions were overturned in 2002. New York City settled a lawsuit by them for $41 million in 2004. The $41 million was based on a formula of $1 million for each year spent in prison.*

> There's always such a rush to judgment. It makes a fair trial hard to get.
>
> John Grisham

They admitted they were guilty. The police doing the original investigation say they were guilty. The fact that that case was settled with so much evidence against them is outrageous. And the woman, so badly injured, will never be the same.

Statement to CNN regarding the exoneration of the five juvenile men convicted of attacking and raping a Central Park jogger in 1989. The men were exonerated in October 2016.

My name is Clarence Elkins, and I served six and a half years in prison for crimes I did not commit.

When I was in prison in Lucasville, Ohio, I had to take drug tests. It was difficult for me to use the restroom in front of so many people. Even though I gave them a sample and passed the test, the sergeant said that I had refused testing and put me in the "hole." The next time, I was put in solitary because I had been having psychological problems. I was hearing people plotting to kill me. I pretty much lost my mind. I didn't get to talk to anyone—they just put me in

solitary until they thought I was OK, and then they let me out and put me right back where I had been.

A couple of weeks later, they put me back in solitary. The last time, I was in solitary for three months. It turned out that the actual perpetrator of the crimes I was convicted of was serving time in the same prison, so they put me in "protective custody" because they thought I might be in danger. I did absolutely nothing wrong, but I was treated the same as everyone else in solitary. I didn't get any assistance from the staff—they would walk right by me like they didn't see or hear me. I felt neglected and completely invisible. I felt like I didn't mean anything.

The noise in solitary is unbearable. Twenty-four hours a day there are inmates hollering and screaming about nothing. I thought I was going to lose my mind one night—I just started screaming too. It's just such a lonely place. It's the worst of the worst. Prison is bad, but solitary is really bad. No visits, no family, limited reading materials, screaming 24-7, terrible food, disgusting showers. Being locked up in a tiny cell that long is cruel and unusual.

When I finally walked out of the prison, some news reporters were out there waiting and someone raised my hand up in the air. I was actually numb. I thought, "OK. This is another day." I didn't think it was real. Coming out of solitary and into society, I just didn't have any feelings when I walked out the door. You don't know what to expect, or what to do. Six years later, I'm still learning how to cope.

Statement of Clarence Elkins, wrongly imprisoned in Ohio for 6 ½ years

I have always heard that the selection and the affirmation of a Supreme Court judge is the biggest thing a president can do. . . . I've always heard that that's the biggest thing. Now, I would say that defence is the biggest thing. You know, to be honest, there are a number of things.

Associated Press interview, April 22, 2017

"When I use a word," Humpty Dumpty said in rather a scornful tone, "it means just what I choose it to mean—neither more nor less."

"The question is," said Alice, "whether you can make words mean so many different things."

> "The question is," said Humpty Dumpty, "which is to be master—that's all."
>
> Lewis Carroll, *Through the Looking Glass*

This great community of nations has something else in common: In every one of them, it is the people, not the powerful, who have always formed the foundation of freedom and the cornerstone of our defense.

Warsaw, Poland, July 7, 2017

> Now I will tell you the answer to my question. It is this. The Party seeks power entirely for its own sake. We are not interested in the good of others; we are interested solely in power, pure power. What pure power means you will understand presently. We are different from the oligarchies of the past in that we know what we are doing. All the others, even those who resembled ourselves, were cowards and hypocrites. The German Nazis and the Russian Communists came very close to us in their methods, but they never had the courage to recognize their own motives. They pretended, perhaps they even believed, that they had seized power unwillingly and for a limited time, and that just around the corner there lay a paradise where human beings would be free and equal. We are not like that. We know that no one ever

> seizes power with the intention of relinquishing it. Power is not a means; it is an end. One does not establish a dictatorship in order to safeguard a revolution; one makes the revolution in order to establish the dictatorship. The object of persecution is persecution. The object of torture is torture. The object of power is power. Now you begin to understand me.
>
> George Orwell, *1984*

Everybody is talking about the protesters burning the American flags and proudly waving Mexican flags. I want America First—so do voters!

Tweet, May 2, 2016

> You may tell the greatest lies and wear a brilliant disguise, but you can't escape the eyes of the one who sees right through you.
>
> Tom Robbins, *Villa Incognito*

When they throw large sacks of drugs over, and if you have people on the other side of the wall, you don't see them—they hit you on the head with 60 pounds of stuff?

It's over. As crazy as that sounds, you need transparency through that wall.

Explaining why the border wall between the United States and Mexico needs to be transparent.

> My mother had always told her kids: if you're about to do something, and you want to know if it's a bad idea, imagine seeing it printed in the paper for all the world to see.
>
> Gillian Flynn, *Gone Girl*

But we are seriously looking at a solar wall. And remember this, it's a 2,000 mile border, but you don't need 2,000 miles of wall because you have a lot of natural barriers. You have mountains. You have some rivers that are violent and vicious. You have some areas that are so far away that you don't really have people crossing. So you don't need that. But you'll need anywhere from 700 to 900 miles.

Interview aboard Air Force One, July 12, 2017

> "Oh, Eeyore, you are wet!" said Piglet, feeling him.
>
> Eeyore shook himself, and asked somebody to explain to Piglet what happened when you had been inside a river for quite a long time.
>
> A.A. Milne

When I travel internationally, I see magnificent places you wouldn't believe. I see properly maintained bridges, tunnels, and airports. I see great highways and unbelievably efficient power systems.

Crippled America

> I can't think of anything that excites a greater sense of childlike wonder than to be in a country where you are ignorant of almost everything.
>
> Bill Bryson

I'll tell you what, do you want to set up the meeting? . . . Are they friends of yours? So set up the meeting. . . . I would love to meet with the black caucus. I think it's great.

Responding to a question from an African-American reporter, April Ryan, about whether he plans to meet with the Congressional Black Caucus. Trump asked if the Ryan knows members of the CBC. When Ryan said she knows some, Trump asked if she could set up a meeting. February 17, 2017

> We have made enormous progress in teaching everyone that racism is bad. Where we seem to have dropped the ball . . . is in teaching people what racism actually is.
>
> Jon Stewart

[T]he flag is much more than a red, white, and blue cloth rectangle. It is a symbol to me, to you, and to people around the world. It represents equality, hope, and fairness. It represents courage and sacrifice.

Crippled America, *2015*

> I prefer someone who burns the flag and then wraps themselves up in the Constitution over someone who burns the Constitution and then wraps themselves up in the flag.
>
> Molly Ivins

I think the big problem this country has is being politically correct. I've been challenged by so many people and I don't, frankly, have time for total political correctness. And to be honest with you, this country doesn't have time, either.

Republican primary debate, August 16, 2015

> If the first words out of your mouth are to cry 'political correctness!' chances are very, very high that you are in fact part of the problem.
>
> N.K. Jemisin

That makes me smart.

Response to Hillary Clinton's suggestion that Trump doesn't pay federal income tax, September 26, 2016

> If anything, taxes for the lower and middle class and maybe even the upper middle class should even probably be cut further. But I think that people at the high end, people like myself, should be paying a lot more in taxes. We have it better than we've ever had it.
>
> Warren Buffett

We treasure the rule of law and protect the right to free speech and free expression.

Speech, Warsaw, Poland, July 7, 2017

> Claire Underwood: We've been lying for a long time, Francis.
>
> Frank Underwood: Of course we have. Imagine what the voters would think if we started telling the truth.
>
> *House of Cards*, Episode 38

This is my exact words. 'I love all the people of our country' . . . They [the media say], 'Is he a racist?

At a campaign-style rally in Phoenix, Arizona, August 22, 2017. Trump quoted his words after Charlottesville to prove that he vigorously condemned white supremacists, the KKK, and neo-Nazis. But he left out the part of his original post-Charlottesville remarks that said, "We condemn in the strongest possible terms this egregious display of hatred, bigotry, and violence on many sides, on many sides. It's been going on for a long time in our country. Not Donald Trump, not Barack Obama. This has been going on for a long, long time. It has no place in America."

> Trust is like a mirror, you can fix it if it's broken, but you can still see the crack in that mother fucker's reflection.
>
> Lady Gaga

Education

Every presidential candidate and every president needs to talk about education. Trump's no exception. But education appears to be an afterthought for Trump. He's not particularly interested in the subject, except as a way to excite his base.

Trump's Education Secretary, Betsy DeVos, is one of several *billionaires* in Trump's cabinet. She decries public schools as a "dead end," promoting "school choice," which is code for taking money away from public schools and giving it to other kinds of schools, including those run by religious organizations. Trump has taken a mostly hands-off approach to education, leaving matters in Secretary DeVos' hands.

No, I'm not cutting services, but I'm cutting spending. But I may cut Department of Education.

October 2015

> As societies grow decadent, the language grows decadent, too. Words are used to disguise, not to illuminate, action: you liberate a city by destroying it. Words are to confuse, so that at election time people will solemnly vote against their own interests.
>
> Gore Vidal

Public education was never meant to only teach the three R's, history, and science. It was also meant to teach citizenship.

In The America We Deserve, *2000*

> This life's hard, man, but it's harder if you're stupid.
>
> Steven Keats, *The Friends of Eddie Coyle*, 1973

There's no failed policy more in need of urgent change than our government-run education monopoly.

September 2016

> The mind once enlightened cannot again become dark.
>
> Thomas Paine, "A Letter Addressed to the Abbe Raynal on the Affairs of North America"

Look at the Department of Education: They're telling people from Iowa and other places and New Hampshire how to educate your children. There's so much waste and we have to stop this.

Fox News interview with Sean Hannity, June 17, 2015

> It tastes like somebody stole my wallet. Ya know?
>
> Gerard Way

We need to fix our broken education system!

February 2016

> It is easier to build strong children than to repair broken men.
>
> Frederick Douglass

We're twenty-sixth in the world. Twenty-five countries are better than us at education. And some of them are like third world countries. But we're becoming a third world country.

June 2015

> There will be statues of Bill Gates across the Third World. There's a reasonable shot that—because of his money—we will cure malaria.
>
> Malcolm Gladwell

Crazy Ideas, Weirdness, Incitements to Violence, and Outright Lies

When we delve into Trump's statements, there are two alternative possibilities for his outbursts and strange utterances, most of which happen on Twitter. The first is that Donald J. Trump is, more than anything else, a little boy with a vivid imagination garnered from staying up late and reading science fiction novels. How else would you explain Trump's idea to place solar panels along the great wall he wants to build between the United States and Mexico? In Cedar Rapids, Iowa, Trump suggested, "We're thinking of something that's unique, we're talking about the southern border, lots of sun, lots of heat. We're thinking about building the wall as a solar wall, so it creates energy and pays for itself. And this way, Mexico will have to pay much less money, and that's good, right?" He added, "Pretty good imagination, right? Good? My idea."

Not really.

The other explanation for Trump's crazy ideas and incoherence is he's not mentally well and not fit to be president. On July 3, 2017, Trump walked right past his limousine after stepping off Air Force One. This limo was at the base of the stairs. He continued to walk, a dazed and vacant look on his face, until he was directed back toward his car by a Secret Service agent. Trump forgot he had just bombed Syria, telling China's president, "We've just launched 59 missiles heading to Iraq." At a Black History Month event, Trump said, "Frederick Douglass is an example of somebody who has done an amazing job that is being recognized more and more, I noticed." Frederick Douglass, about whom Trump spoke in the present, died in 1895.

We have to doubt Trump's mental faculties because not to do so in the face of evidence that he's not capable of discharging the duties and awesome responsibility of his office is a disservice and danger to the United States.

Trump's crazy thoughts splash everywhere and on every subject. Trump doesn't exercise because he thinks exercise "drains the body's 'finite' energy resources," write Michael Kranish and Marc Fisher in their book, *Trump Revealed*. "After college," Kranish and Fisher write, "after Trump mostly gave up his personal athletic interests, he came to view time spent playing sports as time wasted. Trump believed the human body was like a battery, with a finite amount of energy, which exercise only depleted. So he didn't work out."

The Mayo Clinic (like every other medical organization on the planet) insists regular exercise "helps prevent or manage a wide range of health problems and concerns, including stroke, metabolic syndrome, type 2 diabetes, depression, a number of types of cancer, arthritis." This man, the President of the United States of America, is profoundly ignorant and just plain stupid, with the strong likelihood that these two deficiencies overlap.

It's one thing to send 140-character messages, but Donald Trump appears unable to think in details or complexities greater than 140 characters.

If lies were pigs, Trump would have made enough of them to fill a baseball stadium. I've quoted some here, but not all, because they demand a book of their own. (After reading many of Trump's lies, I'm still unable to tell if he's being deliberately deceptive or if he is delusional. Perhaps it's a mix of the two. But what I am sure of is that as a pathological liar, Trump believes most everyone else lies just as often and deeply as he does.

So here it is: The chapter about Trump's crazy utterances, his lies, and more often than not, his crazy lies.

Why can't we use nuclear weapons?

Question posed by Trump to one of his foreign policy advisors, August 2016

> After Hiroshima was bombed, I saw a photograph of the side of a house with the shadows of the people who had lived there burned into the wall from the intensity of the bomb. The people were gone, but their shadows remained.
>
> Ray Bradbury

[Obama] doesn't have a birth certificate, or if he does, there's something on that certificate that is very bad for him. Now, somebody told me—and I have no idea if this is bad for him or not, but perhaps it would be—that where it says "religion," it might have "Muslim." And if you're a Muslim, you don't change your religion, by the way.

March 30, 2011, on The Laura Ingraham Show

> "You're an idiot."
> "I've never claimed to be otherwise."
>
> Cassandra Clare, *City of Bones*

Who the hell wants to speak about politics when I'm in front of the Boy Scouts?

Speech at Boy Scout Jamboree, Glen Jean, West Virginia, July 24, 2017, in which Trump mixed Boy Scouts and cursing.

> I've always been fascinated with the stealing of innocence. It's the most heinous crime, and certainly a capital crime if there ever was one.
>
> Clint Eastwood

Republicans in the Senate will NEVER win if they don't go to a 51 vote majority NOW. They look like fools and are just wasting time.

Tweet calling members of his own party "fools" after the Republican plan to repeal the Affordable Care Act was defeated, July 29, 2017.

> "We're all fools," said Clemens, "all the time. It's just we're a different kind each day. We think, I'm not a fool today. I've learned my lesson. I was a fool yesterday but not this morning. Then tomorrow we find out that, yes, we were a fool today too. I think the only way we can grow and get on in this world is to accept the fact we're not perfect and live accordingly."
>
> Ray Bradbury, *The Illustrated Man*

It's very important, if you have something really important, write it out and have it delivered by courier, the old fashioned way because I'll tell you what, no computer is safe. I don't care what they say, no computer is safe. I have a boy who's ten years old, he can do anything with a computer. You want something to really go without detection, write it out and have it sent by courier.

December 2016

> My needs are simple and few, thought Valentine. Food. Clothing. A comfortable place to sleep. And no idiots.
>
> But of course a world with no idiots would be lonely. If she herself were even allowed there.
>
> Orson Scott Card, *Ender in Exile*

I read a story. It's a terrible story, but I'll tell you. . . . Early in the century—last century—General Pershing. Did you ever hear—rough guy. And they had a terrorism problem. And there's a whole thing with swine and animals and pigs, and you know the story—they don't like them. And they were having a tremendous problem with terrorism. And by the way, this is something you can read in the history books. Not a lot of history books because they don't like teaching this.

And General Pershing was a rough guy. [General John Pershing] caught 50 terrorists that did tremendous damage and killed many people and he took the 50 terrorists and he took 50 men and he dipped 50 bullets in pig's blood.

And he had his men load his rifles, and he lined up the 50 people, and they shot 49 of those people, and the 50th person, he said, "You go back to your people and you tell them what happened."

And for 25 years there wasn't a problem. For 25 years there wasn't a problem. Okay? Twenty-five years, there wasn't a problem. So we better start getting tough!

Campaign rally in South Carolina, February 2016, talking about General Pershing, who was the Philippines governor between 1909 and 1913. Trump told this story five times during the campaign. But the story is utterly false, devoid of even a hint of fact. Not only is it false, but these tactics are now considered to be war crimes. Trump tweeted about this on August 18, 2017, this time claiming that the Philippines was terrorism-free for 35 years: "Study what General Pershing of the United States did to terrorists when caught. There was no more Radical Islamic Terror for 35 years!"

> It was the hat. He looked sweet in the hat. How could a man in a fuzzy blue hat have used human bones to pave his roads?
>
> Jennifer Egan, *A Visit from the Goon Squad*

How low has President Obama gone to tapp my phones during the very sacred election process. This is Nixon/ Watergate. Bad (or sick) guy!

Tweet, March 4, 2017. Trump spelled "tap" as "tapp."

> Better a cruel truth than a comfortable delusion.
>
> Edward Abbey

[America] will be stronger and bigger and better as a nation than ever before.

Speaking to children at the annual White House Easter egg roll, April 2017. To children.

> [Trump is an] odd guy . . . smart with no judgment
>
> Tweet from Anthony Scaramucci, February 1, 2012

His grandmother in Kenya said, "Oh, no, he was born in Kenya and I was there and I witnessed the birth." She's on tape. I think that tape's going to be produced fairly soon. Somebody is coming out with a book in two weeks, it will be very interesting.

April 7, 2011, on MSNBC's Morning Joe

People love conspiracy theories.

Neil Armstrong

His wife, she was standing there, she had nothing to say. She probably—maybe she wasn't allowed to have anything to say.

ABC News interview, July 30, 2016, talking about Ghazala Khan, the mother of Captain Humayun Khan, who was killed in the Iraq War. Ghazala Khan is from Pakistan. Her husband spoke at the Democratic Convention, sharply criticizing Donald Trump. Ghazala Khan did not speak at the convention (though she has on other occasions); she stood beside her husband.

Donald Trump consistently smears the character of Muslims. He disrespects other minorities; women; judges; even his own party leadership.

He vows to build walls, and ban us from this country. . . .

Let me ask you: have you even read the United States constitution? I will gladly lend you my copy. In this document, look for the words "liberty" and "equal protection of law".

Humayun Khan

There was no mix there. That was a standing ovation from the time I walked out to the time I left, and for five minutes after I had already gone. There was no mix. And I got a call from the head of the Boy Scouts saying it was the greatest speech that was ever made to them, and they were very thankful. So there was—there was no mix.

Responding to a question about the mixed reviews he received to his recent speech to the Boy Scouts, The Wall Street Journal *interview, July 25, 2017. During that speech, Trump bragged about his election win, used a swear word—"Who the hell wants to speak about politics"—and made a sexual innuendo. The head of the Boy Scouts did not call Trump to congratulate him on the speech.*

Cop: You know why I pulled you over?

Fletcher: Depends on how long you were following me!

Cop: Why don't we just take it from the top?

Fletcher: Here goes: I sped. I followed too closely. I ran a stop sign. I almost hit a Chevy. I sped some more. I failed to yield at a crosswalk. I changed lanes at the intersection. I changed lanes without signaling while running a red light and speeding!

Cop: Is that all?

Fletcher: No. I have unpaid parking tickets.

From *Liar, Liar*, 1997, with Jim Carrey

Numerous states are refusing to give information to the very distinguished VOTER FRAUD PANEL. What are they trying to hide?

Tweet, in response to near unanimity among states not to deliver to information requested by Trump's election fraud commission July 1, 2017

> Wherever the real power in a Government lies, there is the danger of oppression. In our Governments, the real power lies in the majority of the Community, and the invasion of private rights is chiefly to be apprehended, not from the acts of Government contrary to the sense of its constituents, but from acts in which the Government is the mere instrument of the major number of the constituents.
>
> James Madison, *Letters and Other Writings of James Madison, Volume 3*

Is it legal for a sitting President to be "wire tapping" a race for president prior to an election? Turned down by court earlier. A NEW LOW!

One of several fantasy tweets about President Barack Obama tapping Trump's phones, March 4, 2017

> Reality is that which, when you stop believing in it, doesn't go away.
>
> Philip K. Dick, *I Hope I Shall Arrive Soon*

I saw him at a cocktail party, and it was very sad because the hottest people in New York were at this party.

Speech at Boy Scout Jamboree, Glen Jean, West Virginia July 24, 2017, talking about the developer Louis Levitt. Speaking to Boy Scouts.

> Always the innocent are the first victims, so it has been for ages past, so it is now.
>
> J.K. Rowling, *Harry Potter and the Sorcerer's Stone*

I'll bet if I didn't harass Apple for the last 2 years about the large screen iPhone, they wouldn't have done it—but it bends & breaks!

Tweet, September 26, 2014

> The liar's punishment is, not in the least that he is not believed, but that he cannot believe anyone else.
>
> George Bernard Shaw, *The Quintessence of Ibsenism*

They didn't put themselves down as neo-Nazis. And you had some very bad people in that group. But you also had people that were very fine people on both sides.

Remarks about the white supremacist and neo-Nazi march in Charlottesville, Virginia in which one person was killed and nineteen injured, August 16, 2017

> "Are you a communist?"
> "No I am an anti-fascist."
> "For a long time?"
> "Since I have understood fascism."
>
> Ernest Hemingway, *For Whom the Bell Tolls*

I want to make sure when I make a statement that the statement is correct. And there was no way of making a correct statement that early. I had to see the facts, unlike a lot of reporters. I didn't know David Duke was there. I wanted to see the facts. And the facts, as they started coming out, were very well-stated. In fact, everybody said his statement was beautiful. If he would have made it sooner, that would have been good. I couldn't have made it sooner, because I didn't know all of the facts. Frankly, people still don't know all of the facts. It was very important . . . It was very important to me to get the facts out and correctly. Because if I would have made a fast statement—and the first statement was made without knowing much other than what we were seeing. The second statement was made with knowledge, with great knowledge . . . There are still things that people don't know. I want to make a statement with knowledge. I wanted to know the facts.

Press conference August 16, 2017, talking about his statement the previous Saturday about the murder and violence in Charlottesville, Virginia by neo-Nazis and other racist groups.

> On the throne of the world, any delusion can become fact.
>
> Gore Vidal, *Julian*

You know the catapult is quite important. So I said what is this? Sir, this is our digital catapult system. He said well, we're going to this because we wanted to keep up with modern [technology]. I said you don't use steam anymore for catapult? No sir. I said, "Ah, how is it working?" "Sir, not good. Not good. Doesn't have the power. You know the steam is just brutal.

You see that sucker going and steam's going all over the place, there's planes thrown in the air."

It sounded bad to me. Digital. They have digital. What is digital? And it's very complicated, you have to be Albert Einstein to figure it out. And I said—and now they want to buy more aircraft carriers. I said what system are you going to be—"Sir, we're staying with digital." I said no you're not. You going to goddamned steam, the digital costs hundreds of millions of dollars more money and it's no good.

Time *magazine interview, May 11, 2017, in which Trump pretends to know what's best for the military and demonstrates profound ignorance about weapons technology.*

> I am so clever that sometimes I don't understand a single word of what I am saying.
>
> Oscar Wilde, *The Happy Prince and Other Stories*

Putin & I discussed forming an impenetrable Cyber Security unit so that election hacking, & many other negative things, will be guarded.

Tweet, July 10, 2017, discussing the face-to-face meeting between Trump and Putin at the G20 summit. Hours later, after much ridicule and condemnation, Trump offered a revisionist tweet: "The fact that President Putin and I discussed a Cyber Security unit doesn't mean I think it can happen. It can't-but a ceasefire can, & did!"

> Partnering with Putin on a "Cyber Security Unit" is akin to partnering with Assad on a "Chemical Weapons Unit"
>
> Senator Marco Rubio, tweet, July 10, 2017

There are very few Republicans in Baltimore, if any.

June, 2017, Complaining about his Attorney General Jeff Sessions' deputy Rod Rosenstein, who's from Baltimore.

> You don't make progress by standing on the sidelines, whimpering and complaining. You make progress by implementing ideas.
>
> Shirley Chisholm

They didn't put themselves down as neo-Nazis. And you had some very bad people in that group. But you also had people that were very fine people on both sides.

You had people in that group—excuse me, excuse me—I saw the same pictures as you did. You had people in that group that were there to protest the taking down, of to them, a very, very important statue and the renaming of a park from Robert E. Lee to another name.

Press conference, August 16, 2017

The English language has 112 words for deception, according to one count, each with a different shade of meaning: collusion, fakery, malingering, self-deception, confabulation, prevarication, exaggeration, denial.

Robin Marantz Henig

I love the old days, you know? You know what I hate? There's a guy totally disruptive, throwing punches, we're not allowed punch back anymore.... I'd like to punch him in the face, I'll tell ya.

At a campaign rally in Nevada, talking about how he'd handle a protester, Feb. 22, 2016

The ultimate weakness of violence is that it is a descending spiral, begetting the very thing it seeks to destroy. Instead of diminishing evil, it multiplies it. Through violence you may murder the liar, but you cannot murder the lie, nor establish the truth. Through violence you may murder the hater, but you do not murder hate. In fact, violence merely increases hate. So it goes. Returning violence for violence multiplies violence, adding deeper darkness to a night already devoid of stars.

Martin Luther King Jr., *Where do we go from here: Chaos or Community?*, 1967

For those that don't think a wall (fence) works, why don't they suggest taking down the fence around the White House? Foolish people!

Tweet, August 31, 2015

> No. No. I'm listening. It just takes me a minute to process that much stupid all at once.
>
> Sheldon Cooper, *The Big Bang Theory*

I was sitting at the table, we had finished dinner. We're now having dessert—and we had the most beautiful piece of chocolate cake that you've ever seen—and President Xi was enjoying it.

So what happens is I said, "We've just launched 59 missiles heading to Iraq, and I wanted you to know this." And he was eating his cake. And he was silent.

Describing how he informed the Chinese President of the U.S. missile strike in Syria. (Trump erred in this interview when he said the missiles were launched at Iraq.) Fox Business, April 12, 2017

> It was a movie about American bombers in World War II and the gallant men who flew them. Seen backwards by Billy, the story went like this: American planes, full of holes and wounded men and corpses took off backwards from an airfield in England. Over France, a few German fighter

planes flew at them backwards, sucked bullets and shell fragments from some of the planes and crewmen. They did the same for wrecked American bombers on the ground, and those planes flew up backwards to join the formation.

The formation flew backwards over a German city that was in flames. The bombers opened their bomb bay doors, exerted a miraculous magnetism which shrunk the fires, gathered them into cylindrical steel containers , and lifted the containers into the bellies of the planes. The containers were stored neatly in racks. The Germans below had miraculous devices of their own, which were long steel tubes. They used them to suck more fragments from the crewmen and planes. But there were still a few wounded Americans though and some of the bombers were in bad repair. Over France though, German fighters came up again, made everything and everybody as good as new.

When the bombers got back to their base, the steel cylinders were taken from the racks and shipped back to the United States of America, where factories were operating night and day, dismantling the cylinders, separating the dangerous contents into minerals. Touchingly, it was mainly women who did this work. The minerals were then shipped to specialists in remote areas. It was their business to put them into the ground, to hide them cleverly, so they would never hurt anybody ever again.

Kurt Vonnegut Jr., *Slaughterhouse-Five*

That is a school thing, to a certain extent. I guess you could say it's a hereditary thing, too, I would imagine. It certainly is a hereditary thing, but a lot of schools aren't providing proper food because they have budget problems, and they're buying cheaper food and not as good of food, and the big thing—when I went to school I always loved sports, and I would always—I loved to eat and I loved sports, and it worked, because I could do both.

Trump's answer to an elementary school teacher's question, "How would you go about handling the obesity problem in the country—especially among children—and the fact that many schools are not providing enough exercise and recess time?" on the Dr. Oz show, September 2017

> Could you possibly be a little more incoherent?" asked Olivenko. "There are bits of this I'm almost understanding, and I'm sure that's not what you have in mind."
>
> Orson Scott Card, *Ruins*

You know what I wanted to. I wanted to hit a couple of those speakers so hard. I would have hit them. No, no. I was going to hit them, I was all set and then I got a call from a highly respected governor. . . . I was gonna hit one guy in particular, a very little guy. I was gonna hit this guy so hard his head would spin and he wouldn't know what the hell happened. . . . I was going to hit a number of those speakers so hard their heads would spin, they'd never recover. And that's what I did with a lot—that's why I still don't have certain people endorsing me. They still haven't recovered.

Trump's reaction to the Democratic National Convention, July 29, 2016

> Too much self-centered attitude, you see, brings, you see, isolation. Result: loneliness, fear, anger. The extreme self-centered attitude is the source of suffering.
>
> Dalai Lama

You can't even use the word "Christmas" anymore. Macy's doesn't use the word "Christmas."

The Economist, *September 3, 2015*

> We use Christmas in our advertising, within our stores—cards, gift cards, gift wrap, music, decorations, ornaments, among other ways to celebrate the season such as seasonal greetings by sales associates.
>
> Macy's spokesperson

Hitler wanted to consolidate. He was all set to walk in. But he wanted to consolidate, and it went and dropped to 35 degrees below zero, and that was the end of that army.

Trump's explanation of how Germany was defeated in World War II, The New York Times *interview, July 19, 2017*

> People's ignorance really pisses me off. Stupidity is when you can't help it—ignorance is when you choose not to understand something.
>
> Sarah McLachlan

Well, I watch the shows. I mean, I really see a lot of great—you know, when you watch your show, and all the other shows, and you have the generals, and you have certain people . . .

Answering the question, "Who do you talk to for military advice right now?" Chuck Todd interview, NBC, August 16, 2016

> I find television very educating. Every time somebody turns on the set, I go into the other room and read a book.
>
> Groucho Marx

There may be somebody with tomatoes in the audience. If you see somebody getting ready to throw a tomato, knock the crap out of them, would you? Seriously. Okay? Just knock the hell—I promise you, I will pay for the legal fees.

Campaign rally, Cedar Rapids, Iowa, February 1, 2016

> Violence is a dead end. It is a sign neither of courage nor power to shoot rockets at sleeping children or to blow up old women on a bus. That's not how moral authority is claimed, that's how it is surrendered.
>
> Barack Obama, June 4, 2009

Hey, I watched when the World Trade Center came tumbling down. And I watched in Jersey City, New Jersey, where thousands and thousands of people were cheering as that building was coming down. Thousands of people were cheering.

November 2015. This didn't happen.

> I was just like a pathological liar when I was a kid. I think I just wanted to one-up somebody. Somebody would be like, "Oh, God, my legs hurt." I'd be like, "Your legs hurt? I'm getting mine amputated next week." And that's actually how my mother found out. She came to school and somebody was like, "God, that's such a shame about

Jennifer's legs.'" She made me purge. I had to spill out all of my lies. I was like, "I said that Dad drove a barge, and we were millionaires, and you were pregnant, I had to get my legs amputated, and I spayed cats and dogs on the weekends." Now I can't lie.

Jennifer Lawrence

Everyone here is talking about why John Podesta refused to give the DNC server to the FBI and the CIA. Disgraceful!

Tweet from the G20 Summit, July 7, 2017, to which John Podesta, who ran Hillary Clinton's campaign for president, replied, "I had nothing to do with the Democratic National Committee . . . So there was no DNC server for me to refuse to give." There was no discussion of Podesta or the DNC at the G20 Summit.

I never lie because I don't fear anyone. You only lie when you're afraid.

John Gotti

I felt that I was in the military in the true sense because I dealt with the people.

Never Enough: Donald Trump and the Pursuit of Success, *by Michael D'Antonio, 2015*

> The supreme quality for leadership is unquestionably integrity. Without it, no real success is possible, no matter whether it is on a section gang, a football field, in an army, or in an office.
>
> General Dwight D. Eisenhower

Well I really watch the shows. You really see a lot of great, you know, when you watch your show and all of the other shows, and you have the generals and you have certain people that you like.

NBC's Meet the Press, *August 16, 2015, when asked to name his foreign policy advisors.*

> I just want to retire before I go senile because if I don't retire before I go senile, then I'll do more damage than good at that point.
>
> Elon Musk

Terrible! Just found out that Obama had my "wires tapped" in Trump Tower just before the victory. Nothing found. This is McCarthyism!

March 4 2017

> Pathological liar is absolutely the toughest individual to deal with as a psychiatrist. Because you can't take anything they say at face value. And you can't, you know, fill in their personality. You don't know what's real and what's not.
>
> Dale Archer

An 'extremely credible source' has called my office and told me that @BarackObama's birth certificate is a fraud.

Tweet, August 7, 2002

> Why aren't crazy people content to take over, like, one town? It always has to be the whole word. They can't just control maybe twenty people. The have to control everyone. The can't just be stinking rich. The can't just do genetic experiments on a couple unlucky few. They have to put something in the water. In the air. To get everyone.
>
> I was tired of all of it.
>
> James Patterson, *Angel*

Did you ever see a migration like that? They're all men, and they're all strong-looking guys. . . . And I'm saying to myself: Why aren't they fighting to save Syria? Why are they migrating all over Europe? Seriously.

In Keene, New Hampshire, talking about Syrian refugees, September 30, 2015

> No one leaves home unless home is the mouth of a shark.
>
> Warsan Shire, *Teaching My Mother How to Give Birth*

So we had to get very, very tough on cyber and cyber warfare. It is a huge problem. I have a son—he's 10 years old. He has computers. He is so good with these computers. It's unbelievable. The security aspect of cyber is very, very tough. And maybe, it's hardly doable. But I will say, we are not doing the job we should be doing. But that's true throughout our whole governmental society. We have so many things that we have to do better, Lester. And certainly cyber is one of them.

Presidential debate, September 2016

> Since becoming a central banker, I have learned to mumble with great incoherence. If I seem unduly

clear to you, you must have misunderstood what I said.

Former Federal Reserve Board Chairman Alan Greenspan addressing a Senate Committee, 1987

Look, having nuclear—my uncle was a great professor and scientist and engineer, Dr. John Trump at MIT; good genes, very good genes, OK, very smart, the Wharton School of Finance, very good, very smart—you know, if you're a conservative Republican, if I were a liberal, if, like, OK, if I ran as a liberal Democrat, they would say I'm one of the smartest people anywhere in the world—it's true!—but when you're a conservative Republican they try—oh, do they do a number—that's why I always start off: Went to Wharton, was a good student, went there, went there, did this, built a fortune—you know I have to give my like credentials all the time, because we're a little disadvantaged—but you look at the nuclear deal, the thing that really bothers me—it would have been so easy, and it's not as important as these lives are (nuclear is powerful; my uncle explained that to me many, many years ago, the power and that was 35 years ago; he would explain the power of what's going to happen and he was right—who would have thought?), but when you look at what's going on with the four prisoners—now it used to be three, now it's four—but when it was three and even now, I would have said it's all in the messenger; fellas, and it is fellas because, you know, they don't, they haven't figured that the women are smarter right now than the men, so, you know, it's gonna take them about another 150 years—but the Persians are great negotiators, the Iranians are great negotiators, so, and they, they just killed, they just killed us.

Speech in Sun City's Magnolia Hall, South Carolina, July 2016

> English usage is sometimes more than mere taste, judgement, and education. Sometimes it's sheer luck, like getting across the street.
>
> E. B. White

And, I can tell, some of the candidates, they went in. They didn't know the air-conditioner didn't work. They sweated like dogs. They didn't know the room was too big, because they didn't have anybody there. How are they going to beat ISIS? I don't think it's gonna happen.

Announcing his candidacy for president, June 16, 2015. This speech should have been Trump's shining tribute to the English language.

> The core political values of our free society are so deeply embedded in our collective consciousness that only a few malcontents, lunatics generally, ever dare to threaten them.
>
> John McCain

Too many hollow compliments are not healthy for kids. It is okay to let your children know they are special. It is a part of being a loving parent, but do not overdo it. To constantly lavish praise on your children for every little thing they do is too much. Do not be easy on them. Let your children work hard to gain your praise. They will value it more.

If you over-compliment a child, they start to believe they are entitled to success in life without even trying, but it is not true. When they grow up they will find out that the world is much more difficult than you led them to believe. Then, if they cannot get something right away, they quit.

Quitting is a habit that is hard to break.

Think Big, *2008*

> Parents can only give good advice or put them on the right paths, but the final forming of a person's character lies in their own hands.
>
> Anne Frank

This came up a little bit coincidentally when I was signing the pipeline deals. I'm all signing, I've got them done. And I said, folks, when do we get this deal? And they said, I think it's from foreign lands. I said no good. Who makes it, who makes those beautiful pipes for the pipeline? Sir, they're made outside of this country, and I said no more, no more. So we added a little clause, didn't take much, that you want to build pipelines in this country, you're going to buy your steel and you're going to have it fabricated here.

Trump's statement when, on the fourth day of his presidency, he signed a presidential memorandum requiring that pipelines in the United States be built with American steel. The memorandum does not have the force of law.

> There is nothing more deceptive than an obvious fact.
>
> Arthur Conan Doyle, "The Boscombe Valley Mystery"

Dogs

The last chapter of *Trump Corrected* is about dogs. Trump frequently uses a metaphor about dogs—incorrectly. "Fired like a dog," "got thrown off ABC like a dog," and "choked like a dog," and "sweating like a dog." Anyone who knows even the slightest about dogs knows they don't sweat, save through their paws and nose. Dogs don't beg for money. Dogs don't choke, like Trump said Mitt Romney did. Dogs are loyal and brave.

It's worth noting that all of Trump's dog metaphors are negative, without any appreciation, admiration—and certainly no love—for dogs. Trump portrays both people and dogs as his foe.

Trump's most telling tweet is this one: "Egypt is a total mess. We should have backed Mubarak instead of dropping him like a dog."To drop a dog is a cruel thought.

Soon after Trump was elected, rumors swirled that he would acquire a goldendoodle and name it Patton. But there's still no White House dog. This makes Trump the first president in a century and a half not to have a pet. Until Trump, only Chester Arthur and Franklin Pierce didn't have a pet in the White House. Sixty-two percent of Americans have a pet, but Trump is not among them.

Robert Pattinson should not take back Kristen Stewart. She cheated on him like a dog & will do it again—just watch. He can do much better!

Tweet, October 18, 2012

> The better I get to know men, the more I find myself loving dogs.
>
> Charles de Gaulle

Egypt is a total mess. We should have backed Mubarak instead of dropping him like a dog.

Twitter, December 13, 2012

> All his life he tried to be a good person. Many times, however, he failed. For after all, he was only human. He wasn't a dog.
>
> Charles M. Schulz

Does anyone remember this @BillMaher clip when he got fired from ABC- in fact, fired like a dog! http://youtu.be/97KllcZidKQ

Twitter, January 17, 2013

Why does watching a dog be a dog fill one with happiness?

Jonathan Safran Foer

@georgewillf is perhaps the most boring political pundit on television. Got thrown off ABC like a dog. At Mar-a-Lago he was a total bust!

Twitter, April 18, 2015

Dogs are our link to paradise. They don't know evil or jealousy or discontent. To sit with a dog on a hillside on a glorious afternoon is to be back in Eden, where doing nothing was not boring—it was peace.

Milan Kundera

I hear that sleepy eyes @chucktodd will be fired like a dog from ratings starved Meet The Press? I can't imagine what is taking so long!

Twitter, July 13, 2015

If there are no dogs in Heaven, then when I die I want to go where they went.

Will Rogers

.@BrentBozell, one of the National Review lightweights, came to my office begging for money like a dog. Why doesn't he say that?

Twitter, January 23, 2016

No matter how close we are to another person, few human relationships are as free from strife, disagreement, and frustration as is the relationship you have with a good dog. Few human beings give of themselves to another as a dog gives of itself. I also suspect that we cherish dogs because their unblemished souls make us wish—consciously or unconsciously—that we were as innocent as they are, and make us yearn for a place where innocence is universal and where the meanness, the betrayals, and the cruelties of this world are unknown.

Dean Koontz, *A Big Little Life: A Memoir of a Joyful Dog*

Ted Cruz lifts the Bible high into the air and then lies like a dog-over and over again! The Evangelicals in S.C. figured him out & said no!

Twitter, February 24, 2016

Such short little lives our pets have to spend with us, and they spend most of it waiting for us to come home each day. It is amazing how much love and laughter they bring into our lives and even how much closer we become with each other because of them.

John Grogan, *Marley and Me: Life and Love With the World's Worst Dog*

.@DavidGregory got thrown off of TV by NBC, fired like a dog! Now he is on @CNN being nasty to me. Not nice!

Tweet, March 30, 2016

Dogs are minor angels, and I don't mean that facetiously. They love unconditionally, forgive immediately, are the truest of friends, willing to do anything that makes us happy, etcetera. If we attributed some of those qualities to a person we would say they are special. If they had ALL of them, we would call them angelic. But because it's "only" a dog, we dismiss them as sweet or funny but little more. However when you think about it, what are the things that we most like in another human being? Many times those qualities are seen in our dogs every single day—we're just so used to them that we pay no attention.

Jonathan Carroll

I'm standing at the debate. I'm watching Marco sweating like a dog on my right.

New Hampshire speech, February 8, 2016

You want a friend in this city? Get a dog.

Harry S. Truman

Mitt Romney had his chance to beat a failed president but he choked like a dog. Now he calls me racist-but I am least racist person there is.

Twitter, June 11, 2016

If I could be half the person my dog is, I'd be twice the human I am.

Charles Yu

Afterword

I hope you enjoyed *Trump Corrected* (as much as one can enjoy reading anything written about or said by Donald Trump).

Writing, and the subsequent editing and publishing process take time, and during that interval, I'm sure Donald Trump will have tweeted and said more outrageous, callous, and unintelligible things. How many will matter is hard to say. If you spot anything particularly egregious, send me an email at trumpcorrected2@bestmail.us.

Please continue to speak out against Donald Trump. Call, visit, or write your senators and representatives. Tweet back at Trump. Write op-eds for your local newspaper. Organize demonstrations.

Work hard to undo the damage he's caused.

About the Author

Bill Adler Jr. is the author of numerous books, including *No Time to Say Goodbye*, a time travel love story, *The Binge-Watching Cure*, a short story anthology, *Tell Me a Fairy Tale*, a storytelling guide, and *Outwitting Squirrels*, which *The Wall Street Journal* called "a masterpiece."

He's the publisher at Claren Books, www.clarenbooks.com, a fiction publishing company.

Adler grew up in New York City, went to college in New England, lived for two decades in Washington, DC, and now makes his home in Tokyo.

He's a licensed pilot and unlicensed writer.

Adler's personal website is www.adlerbooks.com. He tweets from @billadler and can be found on Facebook at www.facebook.com/billadlerjr and Goodreads at www.goodreads.com/billadler.

About the Author

Acknowledgements

No book is an island. (Though as king, president, and emperor of this island, I bear full responsibility for everything in *Trump Corrected.*)

I want to thank Sarah Doebereiner, Claren Books' editor, for her miraculous editing and insights and for shepherding *Trump Corrected* through the publishing process.

Chris O'Byrne and Laura Griffioen at JETLAUNCH, www.jetlaunch.net, added many magic touches to *Trump Corrected*, including additional proofing (oh, do I ever need that), production, and putting the book in sync with Amazon.

Mark Bryan, of course, drew the cover art. If you haven't seen his artwork, hop over to www.artofmarkbryan.com.

Laurel Black's proofing and editing smoothed out *Trump Corrected*'s rough edges. She's great, and you can contact her at laurel.black22@gmail.com.

www.ingramcontent.com/pod-product-compliance
Lightning Source LLC
Chambersburg PA
CBHW060959280326
41935CB00009B/764

* 9 7 8 1 9 4 5 2 5 9 1 0 4 *